SQUARE DANCES OF TODAY

and
How to Teach and Call Them

by
RICHARD G. KRAUS
Teachers College, Columbia University

Illustrated by
CARL PFEUFER

Musical Arrangements by
CHARLES LEONHARD
University of Illinois

THE RONALD PRESS COMPANY

New York

To Anne

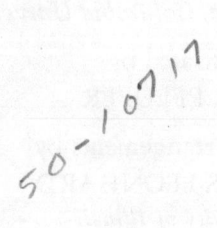

Copyright, 1950, by THE RONALD PRESS COMPANY

All rights reserved. No part of this book may be reproduced in any form, either wholly or in part, for any use whatsoever, including radio presentation, without the written permission of the copyright owner with the exception of a reviewer who may quote brief passages in a review printed in a magazine or newspaper. Manufactured in the United States of America.

FOREWORD

SQUARE DANCES OF TODAY AND HOW TO TEACH AND CALL THEM is an excellent all-around manual for square dance callers and teachers—both those who are already in the field and those who would like to enter it!

Not only does it give full instruction in square dance calling and teaching, but it presents much of the interesting history and philosophy behind this activity that is becoming more and more popular in our schools and communities. Of particular interest is the section dealing with dancing as a tool in community recreation, and with principles of program planning.

Dick Kraus has included a wide selection of square dances old and new, hailing from all sections of the country. These dances, together with the excellent illustrations and accompanying music, make the book indispensible for teachers and recreation leaders who are active in the square dance field.

Dick Kraus has called for and led square dance groups throughout the United States. He presently is in charge of the entire dance program at Teachers College, Columbia University, where he teaches courses in folk, square, social and children's dance. He also writes western comics, the most notable among which are "Monte Hale" and "Hopalong Cassidy"; and he is chairman of the Westchester County Square Dance Association of New York and editor of its publication, *Swing Your Partner*.

CHARLEY THOMAS
Editor, *American Squares*

PREFACE

SQUARE dancing is more popular in the United States today than it has ever been. Already an integral and vital part of the public recreation movement, it is rapidly finding its way into more and more areas of our national life.

Three main factors are largely responsible for this growing acceptance of square dancing by the American public. The first is the emergence of square dance federations and callers' associations and of community and state folk and square dance festivals. The second is the increased awareness that school and college administrators have gained of square dancing as a useful educative technique. The third is the work of a number of outstanding callers, teachers and recreation leaders who, though widely scattered across the country and often working single-handedly, have done a remarkable job of bringing good square dancing to the people.

The appearance of square dance federations and associations and the beginning of community and state festivals has had much to do with what might be called the "revival" of square dancing. Meeting in Kiel Auditorium in St. Louis, the National Folk Festival has drawn many thousands each year to see and hear the colorful dances and songs of Americans of every sort of national descent. Dozens of other state and regional festivals, large and small, have sprung up over the country. The Folk Dance Camp in Wheeling, West Virginia; the Berea, Kentucky, Festivals; the Asheville, North Carolina, Festivals; the Festival of the Nations in St. Paul, Minnesota; the many huge square dance jamborees that are being held annually; all have been a part of this picture.

The California Folk Dance Federation was formed in May 1942, with a membership of sixteen affiliated groups. Under the leadership of Walter Grothe of San Francisco, it has grown until it now includes more than two hundred groups and many thousands of dancing members. Like Topsy, "it just growed." Similarly, California has an active and growing Square Dance Federation. Other federations and associations are springing up in other states and regions, some as a result of California's example, and many others on their own initiative.

Throughout the country—at Columbia University, at New York University, at the Universities of Minnesota, Denver, Wisconsin, Massachusetts and many others—courses in square and folk dancing have become recognized parts of the curriculum. These courses may be given under the jurisdiction of the department of physical education or, in some graduate schools, as part of a separate dance or recreation department.

In elementary and high schools, too, the trend is toward making square and folk dancing a basic part of the educational program. Under the guidance of Robert Hager, the Tacoma, Washington, school system has incorporated it into the physical education program. In all schools throughout Tacoma, square dances are taught to the children. Once a week, a city-wide school square dance is broadcast over a local radio station, with students in all Tacoma schools taking part in a mass square dance in their own gymnasia. As part of the training for this program, schools in surrounding towns and suburbs send groups of children and teachers to Tacoma to learn square dance techniques and to bring these techniques back to their own schools.

In the town of New Rochelle, New York, Gerald Donnelly, superintendent of physical education activities, has regularly taught square and folk dancing in several schools. He has organized an annual exhibition, in which children from the various schools have demonstrated dances of America, old and new, for an enthusiastic audience of parents and townspeople.

Invaluable in this process of spreading interest in square dancing have been the contributions of America's outstanding callers and teachers. The dean of them all is Lloyd Shaw, of Colorado Springs, Colorado. Author of two recognized works in the field, *Cowboy Dances* and *The Round Dance Book,* "Pappy" Shaw has unearthed and set on display many old treasures of American dance. In addition to the hundreds of leaders and teachers who have attended his summer courses in Colorado, he has trained a splendid group of high school boys and girls, the Cheyenne Mountain Dancers. These spirited young performers have toured the country successfully for several years, bringing the authentic dances of the West to the cities and towns of the East.

Perhaps the greatest popularizer of square dancing has been Ed Durlacher of Freeport, New York. He was in charge of square dancing at the New York World's Fair in 1940, has called and taught all over the country, and has worked with many educational and recreational organizations. He has written considerably on the subject and, with the "Top Hands," has made several fine record albums. In charge of a summer program of outdoor square dancing in the New York City parks, he annually introduces square dancing to many new thousands.

Ralph Page of Keene, New Hampshire, known as New England's Singing Caller, is perhaps the foremost collector and teacher of the old Down East contra dances. Al Brundage, Paul Hunt, Lawrence Loy and Floyd Woodhull are other Easterners whose calling has become widely appreciated. Ralph Piper of the University of Minnesota is extremely active as a caller, teacher and organizer of square dance activities. In Texas, Jimmy Clossin, Rickey Holden and Herb Greggerson are three callers who have spread the Lone Star style of square dancing far beyond the borders of that state. Virginia Anderson, twice president of the California Folk Dance Federation, is a key figure in Western square dance activities.

Charley Thomas of New Jersey, editor of *American Squares,* has done much to encourage the square dance movements and to spread word of what has been happening around the country. Rod La Farge, also in New Jersey, and editor of *Rosin The Bow,* has organized callers' jamborees that have brought as many as fifty callers and hundreds of dancers together from all over the East.

Yes, the names are many. But there is still room for many more. Growing as it is, square dancing needs more capable teachers and callers. It needs both recreation leaders and school teachers who want to learn to call as part of their regular job, and specialists to teach and call professionally in community programs, often on a full-time basis.

This book is intended to be a useful guide to the school teacher and recreation worker. Step by step, the process of learning to teach and call is broken down and illustrated in the following chapters. The role of square dancing as a tool in education and recreation is presented, together with the process of building continuing square dance programs.

Complete directions, illustrations and musical accompaniments for fifty-five dances are given. Many of these dances, hailing from every section of the United States, have never been published before. It is hoped that they will prove of use to experienced callers and teachers, who are in search of new dances for their groups.

I would like to express my thanks to Carl Pfeufer, whose illustrations do such a grand job of capturing the wonderful spirit of square dancing, and to Dr. Charles Leonhard, whose excellent arrangements should make the melodies in this book a joy to play—-and to dance to.

Now go to it . . . and good dancing!

DICK KRAUS

September, 1950

TO MUSICIANS

THE piano arrangements in this book have been prepared with two ideas in mind; first, to preserve the folk character of the dances and, second, to keep the level of difficulty within the ability of the non-professional pianist. The keys selected are those that are most likely to suit the range of the caller's voice.

Chords are designated by letters at the beginning of each measure and on all beats where harmonic changes occur. A capital letter indicates a major chord and a small letter indicates a minor chord. For example, D indicates a D major triad (D - F# - A); d indicates a D minor triad (D - F - A); C^7 indicates a C dominant seventh chord (C-E-G-B♭); and c^7 indicates a C minor seventh chord (C-E♭-G-B♭). All chord designations are in terms of fundamental chords, i.e., root in the bass.

Encircled capital letters, e.g., Ⓐ or Ⓑ, designate parts of the dance and do not necessarily pertain to the form of the music.

When small ensembles are used for dancing, the violin or other melody instruments may play the melody, in the octave appropriate to their range, and the piano, guitar or other chording instrument may play the chords indicated or desirable inversions. However, it is recommended that the pianist play the arrangement as written when he is able to do so.

CHARLES LEONHARD

Note: For those leaders who work without live musicians, a list of suitable records to accompany the dances in this book is given on pages 128-129.

TABLE OF CONTENTS

		Page
Foreword by Charley Thomas		iii
Preface		v
To Musicians		ix
Chapter One	THE SQUARE DANCE STORY	1
Chapter Two	THE LEADER'S ROLE	5
Chapter Three	LEARNING TO CALL	14
Chapter Four	THE PATTER SQUARES	20
Chapter Five	THE SINGING SQUARES	53
Chapter Six	CIRCLE AND LONGWAYS DANCES	83
Chapter Seven	ICE BREAKERS AND MIXERS	113
Chapter Eight	SQUARE DANCE PHILOSOPHY	117
Chapter Nine	PROGRAM PLANNING	123
	BIBLIOGRAPHY	127
	SQUARE DANCE RECORDS WITH CALLS	128
	SQUARE DANCE RECORDS WITHOUT CALLS	129
	SQUARE AND FOLK DANCE PERIODICALS	129
	SQUARE DANCE SCHOOLS AND CAMPS	130

ALPHABETICAL LISTINGS
SQUARE DANCES

	Page
Birdie in the Cage	26
Bouquet Waltz	37
Captain Jinks	64
Chase a Rabbit	24
Corners Bow, Partners Whirl	31
Darling Nellie Gray	58
Dip and Dive	68
Divide the Ring	30
Double Sashay	35
Down the Line	36
Duck for the Oyster	20
Elbow Swing	27
Farmer Gray	74
Form an Arch	29
Forward Six and Fall Back Eight	44
Four in a Center Line	45
Gal from Arkansaw	23
Grapevine Twist	28
Hinkey Dinkey Parlez Vous	60
Hot Time in the Old Town (Version I)	56
Hot Time in the Old Town (Version II)	80
Lady Go Halfway Round Again	34
Lucy Long	76
Mill Wheel, The	39
Pass the Left Hand Lady Under	66
Red River Valley (Version I)	54
Red River Valley (Version II)	81
Route, The	42
Sashay and Swing the Girl Behind You	40
Shoot the Owl	38
Suzie Q	43
Swing Like Thunder	25
Take a Peek	22
Texas Star	32
Three Ladies Chain	33
Tucker's Waltz	70
Two Head Gents Cross Over	72
Uptown and Downtown	62
Wagon Wheel	41
When the Work's All Done This Fall	78
Yucaipa Twister	46

MUSIC

Alabama Girl	107
Bingo	93
Bow Belinda	105
Buffalo Gals	97
Camptown Races	67
Captain Jinks	65

Careless Love	69
Chester Schottische	95
Come My Love	91
Darling Nellie Gray	59
Devil's Dream	52
Farmer Gray	75
Golden Slippers	63
Hinkey Dinkey Parlez Vous	61
Hot Time in the Old Town	57
Life On the Ocean Wave	73
Little Brown Jug	50
Lucy Long	77
Mexican Waltz	99
Miss McLeod's Reel	51
Noble Duke of York, The	103
Oh Susannah	89
Red River Valley	55
Shoo Fly	85
Sicilian Circle	101
Skating Away	87
Soldier's Joy	49
Tucker's Waltz	71
Turkey in the Straw	48
Virginia Reel	109
When the Work's All Done This Fall	79

OTHER DANCES

Dance	Type	
Alabama Girl	Longways Play Party	106
Bingo	Circle Play Party	92
Bow Belinda	Longways Play Party	104
Chester Schottische	Folk Dance Mixer	94
Come My Love	Circle Play Party	90
Grand March, The	March Mixer	110
Mexican Waltz	Couple Folk Dance	98
Noble Duke of York, The	Longways Play Party	102
Pattycake Polka	Folk Dance Mixer	96
Oh Susannah	Circle Play Party	88
Shoo Fly	Circle Play Party	84
Sicilian Circle	Progressive Circle Dance	100
Skating Away	Circle Play Party	86
Virginia Reel	Longways Dance	108

SOCIAL DANCE MIXERS

Broom Dances	114
Cinderella Dance	114
Conversation Mixer	117
Heads or Tails	115
Invitation Dance	113
Last Couple Stoop	116
Matching Cards	114
Musical Chairs	115
Orange Dance	115

Chapter One
THE SQUARE DANCE STORY

THROUGHOUT the everyday life of America, the popularity of square dancing is spreading by leaps and bounds. Square dances are featured over the radio and on television screens, in movies and record albums. Throughout the recreation field, square dances are publicly and privately sponsored. YMCA's, youth canteens, church groups, parent-teacher associations, 4-H and grange clubs are all taking it up. Summer resorts often make it part of their social programs, and even night clubs have found it to have a wide appeal.

The question arises: Is this growth in popularity real or synthetic? Is square dancing just a newly-discovered fad, a craze that may soon die out? The best answer comes from the past—a forthright *No!* Square dancing, popular as it is today, has been an important part of American life, ever since the earliest pioneer days.

In colonial times, settlers often gathered together for husking bees, quilting frolics and barn raisings. And, more often than not, once the work was done they turned to dancing. Ralph Page writes that many years ago in Nantucket the annual sheep-shearing was the occasion for a big dance, called the Sheep-Shearer's Ball, which lasted for a full week. Often there would be no special reason for the calling of a dance—just the desire for a good social get-together.

To spread the word of the coming event, a man might stand on the steps of the general store and shout, "Junket! Junket!" When a crowd had gathered, he would give the details of the dance. The selected meeting place might be in the store itself, in a barn, or even in a farmhouse kitchen. When it was scheduled to be held in a kitchen, all the furniture would have to be cleaned out—even the stove. Sometimes only the woodbox would be left for the fiddler to stand in, with plenty of room for his well-rosined bow to scrape away.

Sometimes the music came from a fiddle, and at other times from a fife and drum. Often in the extreme backwoods where there were no trained musicians, the rhythm might come from plain "ratting," or hands clapping in a steady beat. In very religious communities, the minister and his elders frowned upon dancing and secular music as inventions of the devil. When this was the case, the settlers often did what they called singing games or play parties, many of which are still done today throughout the country.

In the last century the dance became a popular part of urban recreation. Polite society found it the vogue, and the finest mansions were not complete without brightly-lit, slick-floored ballrooms. Here the dancers would come in full dress, to take part in the elaborate quadrilles and contra dances that were made up by the dancing masters of the time. In addition, gavottes, polkas, and occasionally a daring waltz would round out the program. Large orchestras were hired to play for the dances, and it was the job of special floor managers to supervise the dress, decorum and sobriety of those present.

As the years passed, square dancing became supplanted by other forms of dancing in cities and towns. The Charleston, Bunny Hug and Grizzly Bear came into their own, and later the rumba, jitterbug and foxtrot, as they are done today. In urban areas the old-time dances were seldom seen, save for a few scattered clubs and societies which kept up their practice.

But in rural sections throughout the country square dancing remained a popular social outlet. In grange halls, barns and fire-houses, the weekly square dance, usually held on Saturday night, was the time for whole families to drive many miles to get together with friends to gossip, and to have fun. Often the people of a village would block off the main street, set up a platform for the band, hook up a string of light bulbs and have their summertime square dance out of doors.

Then, in the 1930's, more and more city people began to learn about square dancing again. Vacationists who spent their summers in the country saw the local people dancing. It looked like fun, so they stepped into a square—and found that it *was* fun! Skiers up in the North Country found that swinging their partners was a good way to keep the blood circulating on frosty winter nights. Many other city people came to be familiar with folk and square dancing by watching the exhibitions of folk dance groups of various nationalities. Two big fairs helped to bring the public to an increased awareness of square dancing. One was the New York World's Fair where, in 1940, square dancing attracted huge crowds, and the other was the Golden Gate Exposition in San Francisco in 1939.

During World War II, with a tremendous need for entertainment and mass recreation for service men who were many miles from home, square dancing received another great stimulus. Soldiers became acquainted with it for the first time in USO halls and in other service clubs. They liked it, and when they got home, they began to take it up in earnest, to start their own square dance clubs, and to learn to call themselves. Today scarcely a town of any size exists in the United States where some square dancing cannot be found. In a number of cities and localities, there is actually a dance for every night in the week!

Granted, then, that square dancing is firmly rooted in the past and that it is being more and more enthusiastically accepted by people today. However, if it is to be used as a part of the educative process or as a tool in recreation, it must be appraised critically, from the point of view of the teacher and recreation leader.

What contributions has square dancing to make, either as part of the school or college curriculum, or as part of the general recreation movement?

Basically, its goals and objectives can best be described under three main headings: physical, social and cultural.

As a physical activity, square dancing is valuable both in the development of neuromuscular skills and abilities and in the maintenance of good physical condition through regular, moderately strenuous exercise. As part of the physical and health education program in high schools and colleges, it is particularly suitable in that it is a noncompetitive, coeducational activity, requiring a minimum of facilities or equipment, in which all may take part.

It has a further advantage in that it develops a skill which will be serviceable in the later use of leisure time, when the student has graduated. Not many people in their thirties and forties are able to take part in strenuous athletics or team sports—but all of them can enjoy a good square dance session.

In a social sense rhythmic movement and dancing have always been a basic part of man's activity. Certain primitive peoples today, when they meet, do not ask, "What tribe are you?" but "What do you dance?"

So, through the ages, dancing has had a basic appeal.

In today's society, it has a double appeal in that, unlike many other forms of passive, spectator recreation, square dancing is a real participation activity. It is not made to be watched, but to be done. All may enjoy it, whether or not they are capable of highly coordinated and refined movement. Young children can square dance; so can their grandparents, and they can dance in the same set. Blind and partially crippled people have been taught to square dance and are able to gain a real sense of achievement out on the floor. More and more is being learned of the beneficial effects of this type of activity among mentally disturbed and badly adjusted children and adults.

Learning to dance and joining together in the same set helps to give a group of people, no matter what their background, a feeling of cooperation and genuine oneness. Ralph Page speaks of the country dance, as the "ideal foreign relation. Here Poles, Finns, Canucks, Swedes, Yanks, Irish and Greeks, mix and enjoy a common folk alliance."

Properly taught and led, square dancing can give the participants a real urge to take on responsibility as part of the group. Further, it can encourage the growth of social confidence by relaxing individual pressures and giving participants the sureness that comes with "belonging," with being adequate and accepted in a social situation.

John Dewey has stated that education is a continuous life process, with the pre-school and after-school periods being as important as the school period, and that it is a major function of education to serve the end of personality development, and to train the child for good social behavior and social control. It is apparent that square dancing can be an ideal tool toward the attainment of these goals, in the hands of the competent group leader or teacher.

Culturally speaking, square and folk dancing help to bring their participants a rich understanding of the past history of the United States, and of its present complex makeup. Professor Otto Lehmann, former President of the International Commission on Folk Arts, has stated this well in his preface to Elizabeth Burchenal's collection of German dances. "Just as the individual is the last link in the chain of his forebears, so every people is the embodiment of an inheritance from earlier generations. A nation, though it bears the imprint of its contemporary environment, can never belie its ancestral origin, for this origin comes to light in its character and inner nature.

"This innermost being of a people—its soul, as one might say—manifests itself . . . in its celebration of festive occasions, in its songs and dances—in short, in all the ways in which it responds quite frankly and naively to the unwritten laws of custom and tradition, thereby lending dignity and substance to the life of the people. There is no people without its folk dances. . . ."*

Professor Lehmann writes of the soul of a people. Americans have a soul, and it certainly is one of mixed ancestry, for they are descended from immigrants who came to this country's shores from many lands.

Nowhere can this diverse ancestry be more clearly seen and illustrated than in American country dances. The most commonly used formation is the square, or quadrille. Supposedly this name is derived from the French, but actually square dances are done in almost every European country. So too, the steps and patterns of the dances have the same varied background—owing a little bit to the Scandinavian, German, French, English, Scotch, Irish—and just about every other nationality one can name.

Together with the richness and variety that result from this mixed ancestry, there are many regional differences in the style of dancing around the country. So, when dancers do a square from New England, Texas or Minnesota, with all the local flavors of the particular section in the calls and in the rhythm, they somehow gain the feeling of knowing New Englanders, Texans or Minnesotans just a little bit better.

When folk dances of European origin are blended into the square dance program, they help to give the participants a feeling of respect and friendship for those of other descents, and an awareness of the contributions they have made to the common culture. It is hard to harbor a prejudice against a person whose folkways one has enjoyed. And, as an old Scot once said, "Ye canna fight a man ye've danced wi'."

But the best and most important reason for doing square dances does not lie in any of these factors. Certainly it is important that square dancing can be a valuable tool in physical conditioning, in personality development, in spreading and stimulating an awareness of the nation's culture. But the clue to its growing popularity does not lie in any of these. Instead, the answer is to be seen in the glowing, happy faces of the dancers—whether they are young or old, city or country people, elaborately costumed, or in rough shirts and dungarees.

The answer is, "Because it's fun!"

*Elizabeth Burchenal, *Folk Dances of Germany,* New York: G. Schirmer, Inc., 1938.

Chapter Two
THE LEADER'S ROLE

WHEN a person first decides to learn how to call square dances, his first question may logically be "How long will it take?" A teacher or recreation worker rarely wishes to undertake a project that requires too long a period of time before he is constructively at work. He has a class or a recreation group that he wants to be able to teach *soon*.

How long does it take to learn to call competently? There is no set rule. Often in rural communities, it may take several years of practice and experience before one is considered a full-fledged caller. On the other hand, many callers have been known to lead and call simple dances, a few short weeks after they began to dance themselves. Summer recreation schools, with speeded-up programs, often teach people to call within a few days of intensive classes. The length of time depends to a great extent on the initiative and interest of the individual. If he is willing to practice steadily, to learn the words of the calls, and to make the plunge without too much delay, then he may start to call very quickly. Of course, that does not mean that he will be a finished caller. Instead, he must constantly be learning, improving his technique, meeting new situations and adding new dances to his repertoire.

At the outset one basic rule must be laid down. Before attempting to lead or call a square dance, it is imperative that the individual be able to dance well himself.

LEARNING TO DANCE

To learn to dance, the beginning caller should take full advantage of the available square dance clubs and groups in his community, by attending them as often as possible. Sometimes he may find that local YMCA's or church groups sponsor regular square dance meetings, with emphasis on instruction and correct technique. Granges and farm youth clubs may have square dances in the vicinity. Colleges and state universities should be queried for available courses on the subject. Sometimes no likely leads can be found at first, and the prospective caller will have to do a little exploring to find a group. He may even have to travel a little, but nowadays it is likely that he will be able to locate a good dance group somewhere in his vicinity.

As the beginning caller gains some dance experience and becomes more familiar with the basic square dance patterns and figures, he will be able to learn dances from record albums and to practice them with his friends. Many albums have booklets of printed directions accompanying them, and some have directions on the records themselves, walking the dancers through the action before the actual music begins. Square dance periodicals should be subscribed to, for through them the caller will learn about nearby festivals and jamborees. Attending these will give him an opportunity to observe different styles of dancing and calling, and to learn a variety of new dances.

But just dancing and having a good time is not enough at this point. For often some person will say, "I've been square dancing for years, but I can't call or teach a dance. I never remember the names of the different squares—or the order of the steps—or the tunes!" This person has a good time dancing, but probably has never made an effort to remember the dances systematically. The person who wants to learn to teach and call squares must do more than just dance. He must be attentive and analytical. He must become familiar with the various dance patterns and sequences, and he must listen to the calls, gradually absorbing them over a period of time.

After learning to dance properly and becoming familiar with a number of different dances, the prospective caller must learn to teach what he knows.

LEARNING TO TEACH

In rural communities where all the dancers know the calls and steps by heart, a caller usually finds it unnecessary to teach a dance before calling it. It is common practice in many sections of the country to go right into the dance without instruction, and often without even announcing the name of the square. So well do the dancers know the calls that they could probably dance just to the music, without a caller! And to city people who are often completely unable to understand the nasal "tobacco chant" of the rural caller, it sometimes seems that that is what they are doing.

But in city groups, in school classes and in the average recreation situation, teaching the dances and organizing a program is a vital part of the caller's job. Each dance must be presented simply, clearly and thoroughly, so that all of the participants can learn it.

During a class session or evening's program, the dances should progress from the most basic and simple movements to more and more difficult steps. At the outset, in working with a completely inexperienced group, it is wise to teach the basic steps: swing, circle and promenade. This can be done either in a large circle of couples, spaced around the floor, or in squares of four couples each. All the sets on the floor should be taught simultaneously by the caller—with all of the participants' attention being focused on him. If there are experienced dancers mingled in the group, they should not interfere while *he* is teaching or demonstrating. Afterward, when their set is going through the figure they may help to smooth out difficulties.

Usually the caller begins by teaching the square dance formation, since this is basic to all of the dances.

THE SQUARE DANCE FORMATION

The square set is composed of four couples standing on the sides of a hollow square, facing in toward the center. Each couple is on one side of the square, with its back parallel to one of the walls of the room. The boy is on the left in the couple; his partner stands on his right side. The distance across the set is about eight or nine feet (Diagram 1).

Several terms will be used by the caller in teaching the group, and these should be made familiar to them at the outset.

Couple means two persons who are partners in the dance. Hereafter,

SQUARE DANCES OF TODAY

Diagram 1. The Square Dance Formation

through the descriptions, they will be called the boy and girl.

Set means each group of four couples dancing together. It may also mean a group of three different square dances done as a unit, as part of the program.

The couple's *station* describes its position in the set. The couples are numbered in a counter-clockwise direction. The first couple generally stands with its back to the caller and the music. The second couple is on first couple's right; the third couple faces the first, and the fourth couple is on the first couple's left. Since the first couple often begins the action, the most experienced couple usually takes this position.

Couples facing each other are known as *opposites*. The *head* two couples are the first and third. The *side* two couples are the second and fourth.

Partners stand side by side in the square formation. The boy on a girl's left is her partner. The boy on the right of her is her *corner*. The first girl and the second boy are *corners*. The first boy and the fourth girl are *corners*.

Here is an effective way for the caller to teach the square formation quickly: ask the dancers to join hands in circles of four couples around the floor. Then ask them to hold their partner's hand. Have them square off by getting on the sides of the square, so they are at right angles to the other couples with their backs parallel to the wall. This will need to be taught carefully only once; afterward the dancers should take the formation fairly automatically. When the set has been formed, tell the dancers to face their partners and to bow to them. Then ask them to turn away from their partners, and to bow to the person on the other side of them—their corners. Have them number off, with each couple holding up hands in turn, beginning with the first couple.

When the dancers have learned the formation, and their relative stations in the set—and it should take a new group only a few moments to do this—they are ready to be taught the basic steps.

THE BASIC SQUARE DANCE STEPS

The basic movements—circle, honor, swing, promenade and do-si-do—are enough for a new group to learn during the first session, in addition to the figures of the individual squares they will do. In the second session, the caller should review these quickly and then introduce further basic movements, such as the allemande left and grand right and left. The balance, star, ladies chain, right and left through, sashay, and two-couple do-si-do may be parts of individual squares or may be called between figures of squares. These are commonly done basic movements.

CIRCLE: All eight dancers join hands and walk to the left, with a light, springy step. This is a walking step, not a skip, slide or hop. Usually they walk to the left, clockwise, for eight steps; and then back to the right, counterclockwise, for eight steps; bringing them back to their home positions.

HONOR: Facing partners the boys bow, bending slightly from the waist, as the girls curtsey. Depending on the locality, this can be more or less elaborate. Sometimes it is a deep formal bow, and sometimes it is as slight as a quick nod of the head. "Honor" is also called "Address your partners."

SWING: The swing is probably the best known simple action, and the one that is the most fun to do. The most common swing is the buzz step. The dancers take regular dance position facing each other. They put their right feet forward (Diagram 2) with the outside of the foot almost touching the other person's foot. Then, pushing steadily with the left foot, which is kept back, and pivoting with very short steps on the right foot, which is kept forward and on the floor, they begin to swing. This can be likened to being on a scooter. The dancers should swing slowly at the outset; when they gain grace and confidence, they can begin to swing faster.

Sometimes the hand-hold may be shifted so that the boy's left hand holds the girl's right forearm, or so that it is lowered to grip the girl's left hand. In some sections of the country the swing is done as a light walking step, but it should never be a hopping or skipping step.

Diagram 2. The Buzz Swing

SQUARE DANCES OF TODAY

ELBOW SWING: A variety of swing that may be done as part of certain squares is the elbow swing. The two dancers link right elbows and swing in a clockwise direction, either with a walking step or a buzz step (Diagram 3).

PROMENADE: Each couple faces to the right and walks in a counter-clockwise direction around the square, until they reach their home position. They may hold hands in a skating grip with arms crossed in front (Diagram 4—left). Or, in the butterfly position, the boy's right arm is placed behind the girl, holding her right hand high, as his left hand holds her left hand in front (Diagram 4—right).

Diagram 3. The Elbow Swing

DO-SI-DO: Facing their partners, each dancer walks forward. He goes around his partner and returns to place. Both the boy and girl move at the same time, and do not turn as they walk around. They pass right shoulders as they move forward and go past each other. They pass left shoulders as they walk backwards to place. Arms may hang loosely at sides, or may be crossed in front of the dancer.

Diagram 4. The Promenade—Skating Position, Butterfly Position

SQUARE DANCES OF TODAY

ALLEMANDE LEFT: All the dancers face their corners. They give their left hand to the left hand of the corner and walk around the corner (Diagram 5). Returning to place, they drop the corner's hand and face their own partner. This is usually followed by the grand right and left.

GRAND RIGHT AND LEFT: All the dancers face their partners. The boys are facing in a counter-clockwise direction, and the girls are facing in a clockwise direction. They give right hands to their partner and walk by her, passing right shoulders.

Diagram 5. The Allemande Left

Releasing that hand, they give their left hand to the next person. They walk by her, passing left shoulders. They continue to travel around the square in the same direction—boys counter-clockwise, girls clockwise—without turning, alternating right and left hands, until they meet their partners again. Each boy takes his partner in promenade position and then promenades in a counter-clockwise direction halfway around the square until they are back in place. This is sometimes called the *grand chain* (Diagram 6).

BALANCE: This can mean one of two things, and it is up to the caller to warn the dancers in advance which of the meanings he intends.

In *Balance and swing,* called rapidly, the boy takes his partner's hand, her left in his right, and steps back for a moment. The two salute each other just as if they were *honoring* each other. Then they step forward and swing.

In the step-swing *balance,* the boy takes the girl's right hand in his right hand, facing her. Simultaneously, they step on their right feet and swing their

Diagram 6. The Grand Right and Left

SQUARE DANCES OF TODAY

left feet across and in front (Diagram 7). Then they step on their left feet and swing their right feet across and in front. They repeat the entire step. Sometimes this step-swing may be done lightly, without the swinging foot even touching the floor. Sometimes, depending on the local style of dancing, the heel may hit the floor hard on each swing. One old New England caller has described it thusly: "As if you were trying to drive a spike into the ground with your heel."

STAR: This is usually done with four persons, either two couples, or four boys or four girls. All four dancers put their right hands in the center and walk around in a clockwise direction (Diagram 8). At the caller's command, they turn, put left hands in, and walk in the other direction, in most star sequences. The hands may rest in the center, one on top of another, or they may each grip the wrist of the person in front of the dancer. The star is sometimes called a *mill*.

Diagram 7. The Step-Swing Balance

Diagram 8. The Star

LADIES CHAIN: Two couples stand facing each other, at least four or five feet apart. As the two boys remain in place, the two girls walk forward. They give right hands to each other and walk past each other, passing right shoulders (Diagram 9). After they have passed each other, they drop right hands. They then give left hands to the opposite boy. He takes the girl's hand in his left hand, and turns the girl, with his right arm around her waist (Diagram 10). They turn as a unit; he

Diagram 9. The Ladies Chain

steps backward and she steps forward, in a continuous smooth motion. The girls now face each other again. They chain across again, and are turned into place by their partners. It takes eight full steps to do the chain and the turn, and eight more steps for the girl to chain back and be turned by her partner.

The ladies chain is an old quadrille and country dance figure that is used in many of today's square dances.

RIGHT AND LEFT THROUGH: Two couples stand facing each other, arms hanging at sides. They walk toward each other, and pass right through the opposite couple in this way: the boy walks on the outside, passing right shoulders with the opposite girl. Each girl walks between the opposite couple, passing right shoulders with the opposite boy (Diagram 11). After they have gone through, the boy turns his partner with the same turn as in the ladies chain, so the couples are facing each other again, with the girl on her partner's right. Then they do the right and left back, turn, and are back in place.

Diagram 10. The Ladies Chain Turn

Diagram 11. The Right and Left Through

SASHAY: Used mostly in Western and Southern square dances, this is simply a sliding step, done to the side. The word is derived from the French term "chassez" and is still pronounced in that way by some New England callers.

TWO-COUPLE DO-SI-DO: One final basic movement is the two-couple do-si-do. This is found mostly in the West and Southwest, and has a number of variations and names, ranging from "do-paso" and "Grange do-si-do" to "docey-doe." These will be described individually in Chapter Four in the squares in which they appear.

THE PRESENTATION

All of the movements just described are basic to square dancing, and an advanced group should be familiar with all of them. However, in teaching a new group, the leader should present only a few of the simplest steps at the outset. Each time the group or class meets the teacher should add new steps and figures, in addition to reviewing those already learned. In teaching beginners, he must remember that what is crystal clear to him, or to any experienced dancer, may be as puzzling as the riddle of the Sphinx to newcomers to square dancing. The caller must explain a figure slowly, step by step, trying to make his words create a clear picture in the listener's mind. A direction should be given more than once, and should be explained in different ways if the dancers continue to have difficulty with it. The caller must never hesitate to demonstrate a step out on the floor, and, if it is a new figure make sure that the first couple in each set walks through it before he begins to call.

A word of caution is necessary here. Square and folk dancing have been ruined for many young people by teachers who saw the activity as simply a cut-and-dried physical exercise, a drill to be run through again and again until perfect. Unless the teacher's sole purpose is to train dancers for a precise demonstration of a dance, or a completely authentic exhibition, teaching in this way is a mistake!

Instead, the effort should be to teach creatively, with emphasis on making the dancing an enjoyable experience for the participants. If the caller knows a story or an anecdote illustrating the background of a dance, he should tell it. He should make his teaching enthusiastic and interesting. If the participants are having considerable difficulty with a tricky movement that is not absolutely essential to the performance of the dance, he should not spend too much time on it during a single session. Instead, he should go ahead with the dance, omitting the rough spot until the next dance session. Repetition and practice over a period of time are essential to thorough learning and retention of dances.

The caller should not be afraid to give his group difficult and challenging material—if he is certain it is within their grasp. It will keep them on their toes and give them the desire for more. The caller must be sensitive to the dancers' needs and abilities and suit the material to these. As he teaches, he will find that the qualities most needed will be thoroughness, the ability to verbally describe action, a good sense of humor, and, above all, plenty of patience.

None of these traits, it may be pointed out, are inborn. All of them, like calling ability, can be developed. So, it is up to the teacher to be aware of his strong and weak points and to attempt to improve himself in order to become a more effective leader.

Chapter Three
LEARNING TO CALL

WHEN the beginning leader understands the rudiments of square dancing, and is able to teach a dance so that it is clearly understood by a new group, he is ready to learn to call.

There are two main types of square dance calls done today: the *patter* call and the *singing* call. In addition, there are other styles known as the *prompt* call and the *chant* call, but they are not as widely done. This chapter deals with the patter call, and Chapter Five presents the singing call.

In the patter type of call, the words are called against the general background of the music, in a sort of rhythmic chant. The caller follows the rhythm and tempo of the music and stays in the same key as the orchestra, but he is free to throw in words, directions and rhyming phrases, or "patter," as he pleases. He does *not* sing the words to the melody, as in a singing call. As a rule, patter calls are done primarily in the Midwest, South, Southwest and far West, and to a lesser extent in the East.

If the beginning caller has carefully observed and analyzed the dances during his period of dancing apprenticeship, he will have seen that the usual square dance is divided into the following sections:

Introduction, or opening call. The same introduction may be used for any number of patter squares. Examples of introductory calls are given on page 17.

Figure or change call. This is the step or pattern of the individual square dance. Usually, a square is known by the name of its figure. Examples are these: "Birdie In A Cage" or "Divide The Ring."

Break call. This comes between the figures and, like the introduction calls, is interchangeable. Examples of break calls are found on page 18.

Closing call. This ends the square. The closing call can be used interchangeably among a variety of square dances. Examples of closing calls are on page 19.

In calling a patter square the caller uses each of these elements. He begins the call with an introduction. He calls the figure. Then he calls a break. He calls the figure again. Then he calls a break again. When the action of the square has been completed, he ends with a closing call. This sequence is illustrated on page 21.

The patter square is a flexible one, in that the caller may use a variety of introductions, breaks and closing calls—and he may change the sequence in which he calls them. It is up to the dancers to keep on their toes and follow the calls.

CALLING THE FIRST SQUARE

The biggest and most forbidding obstacle for the prospective caller is usually the calling of his first square. Often this presents quite a challenge. But he should not let it discourage him, for, once it is met, the rest is easy.

SQUARE DANCES OF TODAY

The wisest thing for him to do is to pick one square, learn it thoroughly, and then just go ahead and call it.

The caller should select a square that he knows well and has danced several times, so that he is certain of the sequence of steps. Then he should learn its calls, repeating the words again and again, until he is thoroughly familiar with them. In addition to the specific figure of the square, he should choose a simple introduction, break and closing call, to accompany it.

Simply being able to recite the calls by rote is not enough. The beginning caller must practice calling them to musical accompaniment. For this he should use, as first choice, a pianist who can play with a good steady rhythm, emphasizing the chords with his left hand. If this is not possible, a square dance record without calls, in 2/4 or 4/4 time, is a good substitute. If neither of these two is available at this stage, he can give himself a simple, steady clapping rhythm with his hands, as he practices calling.

In a patter call, it is necessary to practice staying on key. Simply explained, this means that as the music plays, the caller's voice is pitched to the key it is written in. He does not follow the melodic line, but rather stays with the music in rhythm and phrasing. Usually, a caller's voice finds the key instinctively; however, some callers may need to practice this. Occasionally a caller is heard who does his patter calls in a monotone, with his voice not on key at all, and remaining on the same pitch. This is thoroughly acceptable, providing it does not become droning and uninspiring to the dancers.

When the caller is thoroughly at ease with the calls of his first square, he is ready to go through it with a group of dancers, who will actually perform it as he calls. This group should not be an expert set for two reasons. If they are experienced dancers, accustomed to smooth, expert calling, they will probably be impatient with him, as a beginning caller. Also, since they know the dance so well, they will not present the problem that a less-experienced group would, as far as the need for instruction goes.

Usually, then, the beginning caller would choose an inexperienced group of dancers with which to practice his first squares. They will represent a real teaching challenge, and they will not be irritated if he fumbles, hesitates and has to start over.

At this point some women callers tend to become discouraged, feeling that their voices are not strong enough to be heard by the dancers. However, there are many fine women square dance callers! Among the qualifications a good caller must have, there are many more important than the ability to create sheer volume and noise. It goes without saying, though, that the caller should attempt to get the most out of his personal vocal equipment. As he calls, he should stand with his head up and his chest out, with feet well apart and legs planted firmly.

Easy, relaxed breathing is important to the caller, and the breathing process should be practiced so the caller learns to draw his breaths quickly at the beginning of each line of the call, or between phrases of the lines. The voice should be projected—out! Instead of calling for the dancers directly in front of him, the caller should think in terms of aiming his voice over their heads, at the opposite wall of the room.

While learning to call the caller is urged to avoid the use of a microphone. It is both possible and practicable to call loudly enough for a group of as many as sixty or seventy dancers with one's natural voice, without strain, provided that the dancers are attentive and do not make any unnecessary noise. Further, it is good practice to begin by calling without a public address system, for in many classroom situations, none is available. However, this does not mean that later on, when a microphone *is* available and the caller is working with a large crowd, he should not make use of one. Most callers do to lessen strain on their throats and to make sure that their words are heard throughout the hall.

It is also a good idea for the caller to stand on a raised platform, as this will make his voice more audible and will enable him to watch the dancers more easily.

The leader is ready to go. Several sets are waiting on the floor. After quickly teaching them the proper formation and the basic movements necessary for the square he will do, he explains the first dance and walks the first couple through the action.

Then he calls it for them, keeping his eyes on the dancers, and making certain that they understand and follow the directions. If there is more than one set of dancers on the floor, he should call neither for the most experienced group, nor for the least expert. Instead, he should make his calls suitable in tempo for the majority of the dancers. Otherwise there is a danger that he will speed up the calls for the expert, fast dancers, or slow them up for the beginners.

When he has finished his first call, he should try to get the reactions of the dancers. After listening to their criticisms and suggestions, he should then try, consciously, to improve his calling. He may be too slow, too indistinct, or too fast. He may lack rhythm, life, color. Whatever the dancers say—and he does want to hear their real opinions, not just praise—he must accept in good grace and attempt to improve. If it is feasible, a phonograph, wire, or tape recording should be made of the call. Played back, the recording may disclose faults or good points about the call that the dancers did not point out. After listening to the recording, the caller should analyze it, practice by himself, and then try again.

As he continues to call and gains more and more confidence the leader should begin to learn new squares. Once he is over the hurdle of memorizing, teaching and calling his first dance, the others will come easily.

SUGGESTIONS FOR CALLING

The caller's words should be clear, distinct, loud and easily understood. A good part of the thrill of square dancing lies in accomplishment. If the dancers do not understand the caller, and get confused and tangled up, they may become thoroughly frustrated, and not wish to dance again.

The call should fit the rhythm of the music, if the dancers are to enjoy themselves to the fullest. Whenever possible, calls should begin and end with the phrases of the music.

The important or key phrases in the call should be specially emphasized. That is, a call like "circle left," "swing," or "first couple lead to the right," should stand out above the others. A call that simply provides background with rhyming phrases need not be called so loudly. In the phrase "Up the river, down the lake, meet your partner and promenade!" the one word that is most important and should be called the loudest is "promenade."

The calls should be so timed as to lead the dancers slightly, giving them time to react to the directions and follow them. The caller should always be a second or two in front of the dancers, and he *must* think in advance about what he is going to do next.

The call should be as lively, colorful and enthusiastic as possible. If it is dull and dragging, the dancers will react in the same way. In a sense, the caller is a showman, and his lively spirit should pervade the hall. This does not mean that he should make an exhibition of himself or show off in any way. The dancers must like and respect the caller and think of him as part of a team in which they are the teammates.

If a mistake is made in the call, it is usually not wise to stop and direct special attention to it. This will probably confuse the dancers further and cause them to lose confidence in the caller. Instead, he should get his sets in order quickly, without stopping the dance if it can be avoided, and keep going with the call. A good way is to call "swing and promenade" until the sets are in order.

It must be remembered that the caller is primarily responsible for the success of the square dance class session or recreation evening. If, in the course of a program, anything happens that threatens the success of the activity in the way of distractions or unfavorable conditions, it is up to the caller to do something about it.

It goes without saying that it is up to the caller to be as friendly and pleasant as possible throughout the dance. Correcting mistakes in an irritable or sarcastic manner, or singling out individuals to embarrass them before the group, hardly tends to create the kind of happy atmosphere that is generally associated with square dancing.

PATTER CALLS

It has been pointed out that the caller must know not only the individual figure, or specific action, of the square that he is to call, but also introductory, break and closing calls to go with the figure.

The following pages contain a wide selection of useful introduction, break and closing calls for use with the squares that are presented in Chapter Four. These patter calls have their origins all over the United States and have a good deal of local color in them. The caller may use them as he pleases throughout all his patter squares.

INTRODUCTION CALLS

All into your places, brighten up your faces,
Tighten up your traces for a good long haul!

Up the river, down the bend,
Join your hands, we're gone again!

All join hands and circle south,
Let a little moonshine in your mouth.
You're all going wrong, go back the other way,
Hold your holts and re-sashay.

All eight balance, all eight swing,
Swing your partner, pretty little thing,
And promenade around the ring.

Tighten your belt, pull down your vest,
Swing with the girl that you love best.

Honor your partner, sides address,
Join your hands and circle left.
Reverse back, about a mile,
Lady in the lead and the gent run wild.

First you whistle and then you sing,
All join hands and form a ring.

All jump up and never come down,
Swing your big foot round and round.
And promenade around the town,
Jaybird on the frozen ground.

Ladies join your pretty little hands,
Gents extend your black and tans,
And circle left.
Reverse back on the same old track,
And make your feet go whickety-whack!

Two-four-six-eight, circle left and don't be late.
Back you go with a heel and toe, circle high and circle low.

Swing your partner high and low,
Swing her till she hollers whoa.
Then promenade around the row,
Scratch your heel and save your toe.

Join your hands in a great big ring,
And make your feet go wing, wing, wing!

BREAK CALLS
Allemande Left Calls
Allemande left to the corner you go,
Grand chain eight around the row.
Wave the ocean, wave the sea,
Wave that pretty girl back to me, and promenade!

SQUARE DANCES OF TODAY

Allemande left on your left hand,
Dance right into a right and left grand.
Hand over hand, go round the ring,
Meet your partner, pretty little thing,
And promenade!

Allemande left on your corners all,
Grand chain eight around the hall.
Up the river, down the lake,
Meet your own with a Ford V-8, and promenade!

Promenade Calls
Promenade eight and promenade all,
Promenade around the hall.

Big foot high and little foot low,
Take your own and promeno.

Tap your heel and save your toe,
Chicken in the breadpan, scratching dough.
Meet your gal in calico,
And promenade around the row.

Meet your honey, pat her on the head.
If she don't like biscuit, feed her corn bread,
And promenade!

Ace of diamonds, jack of spades,
Take your own and promenade.

Barbed wire fence and broken down gate,
Walk your girl till you come straight.

CLOSING CALLS
That's all there is, there is no more,
Take your partners off the floor.

That's the end, I do believe,
Kiss the caller before you leave.

That's the end of this old square,
So promenade to a big soft chair,
You know where and I don't care.

Chapter Four
THE PATTER SQUARES

THE following section contains twenty-six patter square dances, hailing from all over the United States. The majority of them are easily-learned basic calls, to be found wherever square dancing is done. Several of them, however, particularly the Western dances, may be classified as advanced and should not be attempted by beginners.

In these pages only the actual figure of the dances has been presented. When calling them before a group of dancers, the caller adds introductory, break and closing calls at appropriate points. The first square, "Duck For The Oyster," illustrates the way in which this is done.

To understand the calls, read the directions. The sentences in the directions are keyed by number to the calls which follow below. For some of the squares where additional explanation is needed, a diagram illustrates the actions. Since these patter calls can be done to a variety of melodies, the dances are followed by simple arrangements of five generally useful square dance tunes: "Devil's Dream," "Little Brown Jug," "Miss McLeod's Reel," "Soldier's Joy" and "Turkey in the Straw" (see pages 48-52). Phonograph records for patter squares are listed on page 128.

DUCK FOR THE OYSTER

One of the simplest and most enjoyable of squares, this is danced all around the United States. As it is presented here, it is accompanied by *introductory, break,* and *closing* calls.

Directions
(1) All join hands and circle to the left, then to the right.
(2) The first couple walks out to the second couple, joins hands with them and circles halfway around to the left, so the first couple now faces the center.
(3) As they continue to hold hands, the first couple ducks under an arch formed by the lifted arms of the second couple (Diagram 12). The first couple now ducks back, still holding hands. (4) The second couple ducks under the arch, and back. (5) The first couple now ducks through the arch, and, dropping the second couple's hands, goes on to the third couple. (6) They circle with them, duck under and back, and raise the arch as the third couple ducks under and back. Then they duck through to the fourth couple. (7) They circle with them, duck under and back, raise the arch as the fourth couple ducks under and back. Then they duck through to their home. (8) All eight swing partners. All eight allemande left with corners and do a grand right and left. Meet partners and promenade. (9) The second couple now leads to the right and goes through the "Duck For The Oyster" figure with each couple in turn, going through the action from (2) through (7). The swing, allemande left

SQUARE DANCES OF TODAY

and grand right and left are repeated after the second couple has gone through the figure, and, in turn, after the third and fourth couples have gone through it. (10) At the end, all swing and promenade.

Calls

INTRODUCTION
(1) All join hands and circle south,
   Let a little moonshine in your mouth.
   You're all going wrong, go back the other way,
   Hold your holts and re-sashay.

FIGURE
(2) First couple out to the couple on the right,
   Circle four for half the night.
(3) Duck for the oyster, duck!
(4) Dive for the clam, dive!
(5) Duck on through and on to the next.
(6) Circle four for half the night.
   Duck for the oyster, duck!
   Dive for the clam, dive!
   Duck on through and on to the next.
(7) Circle four for half the night.
   Duck for the oyster, duck!
   Dive for the clam, dive!
   Duck on through and home you go.

BREAK
(8) All eight balance, all eight swing.
   Swing your partner, pretty little thing.
   Allemande left to the corner you go,
   Grand chain eight around the row.
   Wave the ocean, wave the sea,
   Wave that pretty girl back to me, and promenade!

Diagram 12. Duck for the Oyster

(9) At this point the second couple leads out with the figure, to calls (2) through (7). The break call (8) is repeated after the second couple completes the figure. Each couple in turn does the figure, and, each time, when they have completed it, the break call is done.

CLOSING
(10) Swing your partner high and low,
   Swing her till she hollers whoa.
   That's the end of this old square,
   So promenade to a big soft chair.

TAKE A PEEK

Another widely done square, with more than a little bit of play in it. Like "Duck For The Oyster," this square follows a common pattern—that of the visiting couple, in which each couple leads out in turn and visits the other couples, one by one.

Directions

(1) First couple walks to the couple on the right and faces them, not holding hands. (2) The first girl steps to the right of the second couple, as the first boy steps to the left of them. Without going around them, the first girl and boy lean out past them and take a peek (Diagram 13). (3) First couple goes back to the center of the set and swings there. (4) They separate again and take a peek again, around the second couple. (5) They return to the center and now both couples swing. (6) The first couple now goes to the third and repeats the figure with them. They go to the fourth then, and do the figure with them.

Diagram 13. Take a Peek

Calls

(1) First couple out to the couple on the right,

(2) Go round that couple and take a little peek.

(3) Back to the center and swing your sweet.

(4) Go round that couple and peek once more.

(5) Back to the center and swing all four.

(6) On to the next!

Repeat calls from (2) to (5).

GAL FROM ARKANSAW

When a blizzard's in the making and the wind is howling in the rafters, try this to get warmed up. It's practically all swinging; an ideal square for lumberjacks, football players . . . and, oh yes, you and me! Very much like the square called "Swing Old Adam."

Directions
(1) First boy leads to the second couple. (2) He swings the second girl. (3) He then swings the second boy, either with an elbow swing, or in a regular swing position. (4) He returns home and swings his own. (5) He crosses to the third couple and swings the third girl. (6) He swings the third boy. (7) He goes home and swings his partner. (8) He swings the fourth girl. (9) He swings the fourth boy. (10) Returning home, he swings his own, and everybody swings.

Calls
(1) First gent out to the couple on the right.
(2) Swing your maw,
(3) And now your paw,
(4) And now the gal from Arkansaw.
(5) Cross the hall and swing old grandmaw,
(6) And now old grandpaw,
(7) And now the gal from Arkansaw.
(8) On to the last and swing your mother-in-law,
(9) And now your father-in-law,
(10) And now the gal from Arkansaw, And everybody swing!

CHASE A RABBIT

Here is a figure often found in Southern running sets, although it is done as a square all over the country. Basically, the couple walks through a simple figure eight pattern.

Directions
(1) First couple walks to the right and faces the second couple. (2) The first girl takes the lead, and the boy follows directly behind her. She goes through the second couple, dividing them, around the girl and back to the center (Diagram 14). (3) She goes through them again, around the second boy, and back to the center. The first boy has followed her through this. (4) The first boy now takes the lead, and the first girl follows behind him. He splits the second couple, goes around the girl and back to the center. (5) Now he goes through them again, around the boy and back to the center. (6) Both couples now join hands and circle left. (7) First couple leaves the second and goes on to repeat the figure with the third couple and then with the fourth.

Calls
(1) First couple out to the couple on the right,
(2) Chase a rabbit, chase a squirrel,
(3) Chase a pretty girl round the world.
(4) Now that possum, now that coon,
(5) Now that big boy round the moon.
(6) Buckle up four with a two-pair whirl.
(7) Leave that couple, on to the next!
(*Repeat calls from (2) to (7) with each couple in turn.*)

Diagram 14. Chase a Rabbit

SWING LIKE THUNDER

This one goes under a variety of names. Some call it the "California Fruit Basket" and others call it "Ladies Bow, Gents Bow Under."

Directions
(1) First couple walks to the right. (2) They join hands with the second couple and circle left with them. (3) The two boys join hands with each other, and the two girls do the same, under the boys' hands (Diagram 15). (4) The boys lift their hands over the girls' heads and drop them, still joined, behind their backs. (5) The girls lift their hands over the boys' heads and drop them behind their backs. An interlocking basket of four people is formed. (6) The dancers put their right feet forward and, pushing with their left feet, just as in the buzz swing, circle to the left (Diagram 16). They begin slowly and pick up speed gradually. (7) They drop hands and circle left with the same couple. (8) The first couple leaves that couple and goes on to the third. They repeat the figure with them, and then with the fourth.

Calls
(1) First couple out to the couple on the right.
(2) Circle four for half the night.
(3) Hands across!
(4) Ladies bow!
(5) Gents bow under!
(6) Hold your holts and swing like thunder.
(7) Drop your hands and circle four,
(8) Leave that couple and pass right o'er. On to the next!

Diagram 15. Swing Like Thunder

Diagram 16. Swing Like Thunder

Variation—In a second version of this dance, the first couple, instead of leaving the second, circles with them, and then adds the third couple, making it a circle of six people. They do the basket with three couples. Then they add the fourth couple, and do the basket with all eight people dancing.

BIRDIE IN THE CAGE

One of the most popular square dance calls, this visiting-couple square is done all over the country.

Directions
(1) First couple leads to the couple on the right. They join hands with them and circle to the left. (2) The first girl drops the hands of the others and the other three circle to the left around her. As they do this, she turns in the opposite direction, to the right, inside their circle. (3) The first girl now steps out of their circle and joins hands with the second couple, as the first boy steps into the center. They circle three hands around him, and he turns in the reverse direction. (4) The first boy now steps out of the ring and swings his partner. Both couples swing. (5) The first couple now repeats the figure with each of the other couples in turn.

Calls
(1) First couple out to the couple on the right.
Circle four for half the night.
(2) Birdie in the cage, three hands round,
Make that big foot jar the ground.
(3) Birdie fly out, the crow hop in,
Hang that buzzard from a high old limb.
(4) Crow hop out and swing your own.
Both couples swing,
(5) And lead to the next!

ELBOW SWING

In this square the action is not at all difficult, but the timing is very exact. This is a real test of the caller's ability to keep all the sets doing the same thing at the same time.

Directions

(1) The first boy walks toward the second boy, who comes out to meet him. (2) They link right elbows and swing one and a half times around. (3) Letting go of each other, each goes to the other boy's partner, the first boy to the second girl, and the second boy to the first girl. (4) Joining left elbows with this new girl, each swings her one time around, so the boys are facing the center again. (5) The two boys swing again with right elbows joined, one and a half times around. (6) Leaving each other, each swings his own partner with left elbows linked, once around. (7) The first boy now goes to the third couple and repeats the figure with them, and then with the fourth couple.

Calls
(1) First gent out to the couple on the right.
(2) Two gents swing with a right elbow,
(3) Once and a half!
(4) Opposite lady with a left elbow,
Once around!
(5) Two gents swing with a right elbow,
Once and a half!
(6) Now your own with a left elbow,
Once around!
(7) Lead to the next.

Additional patter
Two gents swing with a hook and a swing,
Opposite lady with a turkey wing.
Two gents swing with the same old thing,
And now your own with a pigeon wing!

GRAPEVINE TWIST

This is an add-on square, in which one couple leads out and gradually picks up the other couples, until the entire set is dancing as a unit. With a lively crowd dancing, this square can become like the ice-skating game, "crack the whip." It should be toned down if it becomes too boisterous.

Directions
(1) The first boy takes his partner's left wrist in his right hand. (2) With the boy in the lead and the girl following, they go to the second couple and go through them. (3) They cut to the left, around the second girl, and back to the center (Diagram 17). (4) Going straight into the center, the boy then turns to his right, with his partner still following him. He goes through the second couple again, and now cuts to the right, and goes around the second boy and back to the center. (5) The two couples join hands and circle to the left. (6) The first boy now lets go of the second girl's hand, so a line of four is formed, with the other three following him. He goes to the third couple and does the entire figure with them. He adds them to the line. With six in line, he goes to the fourth couple, and does the figure with them. All eight then swing partners and promenade.

Calls
(1) First gent, take your lady by the wrist,
(2) Round that lady with a grapevine twist.
(3) Back to the center with a whoa-haw-gee,
(4) And around the gent from Tennessee.
(5) Circle up four in the middle of the floor,
(6) On to the next and dance some more!

Note—*The call repeats each time, except that the next time the caller says, "circle up six," and then "circle up eight."*

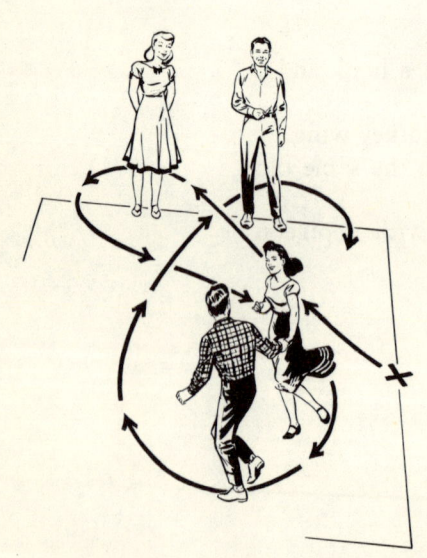

Diagram 17. Grapevine Twist

FORM AN ARCH

Easy to do, but somewhat novel in its pattern, is this changing-partners dance.

Directions

(1) The head two couples, the first and third, holding partners' hands, take four steps forward, then four steps back to place. (2) The same two couples take four steps forward and join their free hand with the free hand of the opposite person, holding the hands high, to form an arch. (3) The side two girls now slide through this arch, leading with their right feet, and passing each other back to back (Diagram 18). (4) All four boys now swing their opposite girls. The head boys swing the girl they have been facing, and whose hand they have been holding up in the arch. The side two boys swing the girl who has come through the arch to them. (5) They swing this girl back to the boy's home position. Then they all promenade around the set with their new partners, to the boy's home position. (6) The action of (1) through (5) is repeated, at the end of which all partners have returned to their original positions. (7) Then the entire dance is repeated, with the *side* couples going forward and back and forming the arch, as the head girls slide through.

Calls

(1) Head two couples forward and back,
(2) Forward again with your hands up high.
Form an arch against the sky.
(3) Side two girls you slide right through.
(4) Swing the gent that's facing you.
(5) Swing 'em high and swing 'em low, And promenade the outside row.
(6) Head two couples forward and back, Forward again with your hands up high.
Form an arch against the sky.
Side two girls you slide right through.
Swing the gent that's facing you.
Swing 'em high and swing 'em low, And promenade the outside row.
(7) Side couples ready!

Diagram 18. Form an Arch

DIVIDE THE RING

This square introduces a step common to many different dances—that of "dividing the ring," in which one couple walks down the set and passes through the opposite couple.

Directions

(1) The first couple bows and then swings, once or twice around. (2) They walk down the center of the set and "split" the opposite, or third, couple, which separates to let them through (Diagram 19, Arrow A). (3) The first couple now separates. The girl goes around the outside of the set to the right and back to her home position, as the boy goes to the left and back to his home. (4) They meet in their home position and swing again. (5) They go down the set again. The boy cuts to the left, between the third and fourth couples, as the girl goes to the right, between the second and third couples (Arrow B). (6) They meet and swing in their home positions. (7) They go down the set again. The boy goes to the left, dividing the fourth couple and returning to place, as the girl goes to the right, dividing the second couple and returning home (Arrow C). (8) Everybody swings.

Calls

(1) First couple bow, first couple swing,
(2) Down the set and divide the ring.
(3) Lady go gee and gent go haw,
(4) Swing when you meet as you did before.
(5) Down the set and cut off four.
(6) You swing her and she'll swing you,
(7) Down the set and cut off two.
(8) All eight swing!

Diagram 19. Divide the Ring

CORNERS BOW, PARTNERS WHIRL

Here is another "divide the ring" figure, with a quick change of partners. This is a long square, with plenty of fast swinging.

Directions

(1) First couple bows and then swings. (2) The first couple walks down the center of the set and divides the third couple. The first girl goes to the right, walking around the outside of the set and back to her home position, as the first boy walks to the left and back to his home position. (3) All the dancers in the set bow to their corners. They turn and swing partners—just two quick swings. (4) They turn away from partners, take corners in promenade position. They promenade so that the boy moves one quarter of the way around the set, or one position to the right. The first boy is now in the second couple's position, and he has the fourth girl for his new partner. (5) The action of (2) through (4) is repeated three more times. Each time the first boy and his new partner walk down the center of the set, divide the opposite couple, separate, and walk around the set to their new home position. All of the boys then honor corners, swing partners, and promenade corners one position to the right. When the action has been done four times, the dancers have all returned to their original position and partners. Each couple does the figure in turn.

Calls
(1) First couple bow, first couple swing,
(2) Down the set and divide the ring.
   Lady go gee, gent go haw.
(3) Corner bow, partners whirl,
(4) All run away with the corner girl.
(5) First old gent with a brand new Jane,
   Down the set and divide the lane.
   Corners bow, partners whirl,
   All run away with the corner girl.

   First old gent with a brand new sweet,
   Down the set and shuffle your feet.
   Corners bow, partners whirl,
   All run away with the corner girl.

   First old gent for the last old time,
   Down the set and divide the dime.
   Corners bow, partners whirl,
   All run away with the corner girl.

TEXAS STAR

The brand says this dance comes from the Lone Star State, but it's actually done all over the country, just about as it's outlined here. A good-looking exhibition figure, and one that's fun to do!

Directions

(1) All four girls take four steps to the center, clap hands on the fourth step, and then take four steps backward to place. (2) All four boys walk to the center, form a right-hand star, and walk about eight steps in a clockwise direction. (3) They take their right hands out and form a left-hand star, reversing direction. (4) Keeping their left hand in the star, they walk past their partners, and take the next girl with their right arm around her waist (Diagram 20). The number one boy has the number two girl, and so on. They walk approximately eight steps in a counter-clockwise direction. (5) The boys keep their right arm around the girl's waist, but drop left hands. The couples now turn, with the girls walking forward and into the center, and the boys backing up to the outside. The girls form a right hand star and walk clockwise. (6) All four boys swing their new partners and promenade them to the boys' home positions. The whole dance is repeated three times more. Each time the boys take new partners until, at the end, they have their original partners back.

Calls

(1) Ladies to the center and back to the bar.
(2) Gents go in with a right hand star.
(3) Right hand out, left hand back, make your feet go whickety-whack.
(4) Meet your partner, pass her by, Take the next one on the fly.
(5) Gents swing out, girls swing in, Form your Texas Star again.
(6) Break and swing that new girl round, And promenade around the town.

Diagram 20. Texas Star

THREE LADIES CHAIN

In this variation of the ladies chain figure, three couples are kept active at the same time.

Directions

(1) The first couple walks to the second couple, joins hands with them and circles completely around to the left, so the first couple stands in the center, facing the second couple. (2) The first girl and the second girl do the ladies chain (Diagram 21). (3) The first boy takes the second girl, turns halfway with her, and turns her on to the fourth girl. The second and fourth girls do the ladies chain. The first boy takes the fourth girl, turns her and has her do the ladies chain with the first girl. He continues to chain the three girls across the set, turning halfway to his left each time he chains a new girl. Each time the second and fourth boys chain a girl, they turn completely with them. (4) When each girl is back with her original partner, the first couple leads to the third couple. They circle to the left with them. Still holding hands with them, they do the "Duck For The Oyster" figure (see page 20). Then they duck on through to the fourth couple. (5) They circle four hands completely around with them, and then do the three ladies chain figure again, with the first, fourth and second girls active. When each girl is back with her partner, the first couple returns home. Each couple leads out to do the figure in turn.

Calls

(1) First couple out and circle four.
(2) Three ladies chain right down the lane,
(3) Turn 'em round and keep on chaining.
Chain 'em in and chain 'em out,
Chain the ocean wave about!
(4) You've got your own so lead to the next.
Circle four in a tight little ring.
Duck for the oyster, duck!
Dive for the clam, dive!
Duck on through and on to the next.
(5) Circle four with the fourth couple.
Three ladies chain right down the lane.
Turn 'em round and keep on chaining.
Chain 'em in and chain 'em out,
Chain the ocean wave about.
You've got your own, so home you go!

Diagram 21. Three Ladies Chain

LADY GO HALFWAY ROUND AGAIN

This is not a difficult square, but for a few moments the active boy has to keep his ears open, and do some fast stepping!

Directions

(1) First couple bows and swings. (2) First couple promenades around the outside of the ring to the right, once around the square, until they are back in place. (3) The first boy stands there as the first girl continues around the set alone, until she reaches the third boy. (4) She takes his left hand in her right hand and joins the third couple in a line of three, facing the first boy (Diagram 22). (5) This line of three takes four short steps forward, four steps backward, four forward, and stands there. (6) The first boy walks toward the second girl, joins right hands with her, and walks around her. (7) He walks across the set to the fourth girl and walks around her, holding left hands. (8) He turns the opposite, or third girl, holding both hands. (9) He takes his partner and swings her across the set into their home position.

Calls

(1) First couple bow, first couple swing,
(2) Promenade around the ring.
(3) Lady go halfway round again.
(4) Join the opposite couple.
(5) Three come forward,
Three step back,
Three come forward and there stand pat.
(6) Lone gent out to the lady on the right with a right hand round.
(7) Lady on the left with a left hand round.
(8) Opposite lady with both hands round.
(9) Swing your partner, swing her home, And everybody swing his own!

Diagram 22. Lady Go Halfway Round Again

DOUBLE SASHAY

This fast-moving square makes use of the sashay, or slide step. The calls come continuously, and there is no pause in the action.

Directions

(1) The first girl and the third boy take four steps toward each other, and four steps back to their home positions. (2) The same two people now walk forward across the set, passing each other and exchanging positions. (3) The first and third girls now face each other and join both hands, with their arms extended wide, and standing close to each other. The two boys face each other, hands at sides, and take a half step backward. (4) They now take eight sliding steps across the set, with the girls sliding between the boys (Diagram 23). The boys slide at the same time as the girls! (5) They have crossed the set. Now the girls drop hands and step back half a step, as the boys join hands in the sashay position. They sashay eight steps back across the set, with the boys passing between the girls. (6) The first girl and the third boy take four steps forward and back. They now cross over, returning to their home positions. (7) All the dancers do an allemande left with their corners, and promenade their partners once around the set and back to place. The dance is repeated three more times, each time with a new girl and her opposite boy beginning the figure.

Calls
(1) First girl and opposite gent,
    Forward and bow and back again.
(2) Forward now and cross right o'er.
(3) Join your hands!
(4) Double sashay,
    Girls on the inside!
(5) Double sashay,
    Gents on the inside!
(6) Same two, forward and bow and back again.
    Forward now and cross right o'er.
(7) Allemande left on your left hand,
    Promenade partners round the land.

Diagram 23. Double Sashay

DOWN THE LINE

Originally a Western call, this square is done—with slight variations—all around the country today.

Directions

(1) First couple bows and swings. (2) First couple now separates, with the girl walking to the right around the square and the first boy to the left. (3) The first girl takes the free hand of the third boy, as the first boy takes the free hand of the third girl. They form a line of four, facing the first couple's home position. (4) This line of four takes four steps forward, four steps back, four steps forward, and stands there, across the center of the set. (5) The side couples become active. They separate and walk up the line, with the side girl on the right of it, and the side boy on the left (Diagram 24). They meet the opposite person at the middle of the line, and swing that person there. (6) Leaving the opposite person, they continue walking in the direction they were going in, and meet their partners at the end of the line. They swing there. (7) Continuing around the line, they meet the opposite person at the middle of the line and swing there. (8) They leave this person, continue down the line and meet their partners in their home positions. They swing there. (9) The first and third couples now join hands and circle to the left. The first couple now ducks through an arch formed by the third couple and returns home. Each couple does the figure in turn.

Calls

(1) First couple bow, first couple swing.
(2) Separate around the ring—
Lady go si and gent go do.
(3) Join the opposite in a line of four.
(4) Forward four and fall back four,
Forward four and there stand pat.
(5) Side two couples down the line.
Swing the opposite round and round.
(6) Keep on going and swing your own.
(7) Round the bend and swing your opposite.
(8) Run along home and swing your own.
(9) The center four circle four,
Active couple duck on o'er.

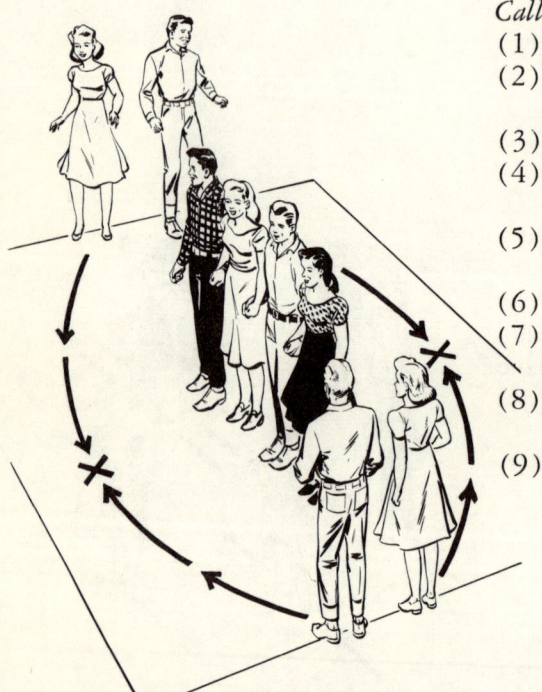

Diagram 24. Down the Line

BOUQUET WALTZ

Far from being the stately waltz that its name suggests, this is a spirited dance that can sometimes resemble a tug of war. As in "Grapevine Twist," the caller must prevent his dancers from becoming too boisterous.

Directions

(1) The first girl walks to the second couple, joins hands with them and circles once to the left with them. (2) Leaving them, she walks on to the third couple and joins hands with them. At the same time, the first boy goes to the second couple and joins hands with them. There are now two circles of three. These two circles revolve around each other in a counter-clockwise direction (long arrows) at the same time continuing to circle to the left in their own circles (short arrows). The purpose is to see how close they can come to the other circle as they revolve around them, without actually touching them (Diagram 25). They go around once at a rapid pace. (3) The first girl now goes on to the fourth couple, as the first boy goes to the third. They form two sets of three again. Again the two sets of three revolve around each other. (4) The girl remains with the fourth couple, and the first boy joins her there, forming a set of four people. At the same time, the second and third couples also join hands, forming a circle of four people. (5) The two sets of four now revolve around each other. (6) All wind up in home positions and swing there. The step through the dance is *not* a waltz, but a regular walking step!

Calls

(1) First lady out to the couple on the right,
And circle three hands round.
(2) Lady go on and the little boy follow.
Three by three across the floor,
Three by three with a Bouquet Waltz.
(3) Lady go and the little boy follow.
Three by three across the floor,
Three by three with a Bouquet Waltz.
(4) Lady stand pat and the little boy follow.
Form your sets of four.
(5) Four by four across the floor,
Four by four with a Bouquet Waltz.
(6) Home you go and swing your own!

Diagram 25. Bouquet Waltz

SHOOT THE OWL

This dance is popular throughout the Southwest, particularly in Texas. It is similar to "Bouquet Waltz" in that it has a follow-up pattern, with the first boy leading out, and the first girl following him.

Directions

(1) All do-si-do with corners, and then with partners. (2) The dancers then do an allemande left and a grand right and left. They meet their partners and promenade home. (3) The first couple bows and swings. The first boy then walks to the second couple, joins hands with them and circles left with them. (4) The second couple raises their hands in an arch. The first boy ducks through this arch, and leaves them. (5) He returns to his partner and swings her in the center of the set. (6) The first boy now goes on to the third couple and circles three hands around to the left with them. At the same time, the first girl goes to the second couple and circles to the left with them. (7) Simultaneously, the first boy and first girl duck through their respective arches, meet in the center and swing. (8) The first boy now goes to the fourth couple, as the first girl goes to the third. They circle, duck through the arches, meet in the center and swing. (9) The first boy goes home and waits, as the first girl continues on alone. She circles with the fourth couple, ducks through their arch and returns home, to swing with the first boy.

Calls

(1) All around your left hand lady,
 See saw your pretty little taw.
(2) Swing on the corner like swinging on a gate,
 Right to your own and a grand chain eight.
 Meet your partners, promenade all!
(3) First old couple, balance and swing,
 Gent lead out for a three hand ring.
(4) Circle around, let out a howl,
 Raise the arch and shoot the owl.
(5) Meet in the center and there you swing,
(6) Both go on for a three hand ring.
(7) Circle around, let out a howl,
 Raise an arch and shoot the owl.
 Meet in the center and there you swing.
(8) Both go on for a three hand ring.
 Circle around, let out a howl,
 Raise the arch and shoot the owl.
 Meet in the center and there you swing.
(9) Lady go on for a three hand swing.
 Circle around, let out a howl,
 Raise an arch and shoot the owl.
 Home you go and there you swing!

THE MILL WHEEL

Here is a dance originated by Charley Thomas of Woodbury, New Jersey. It has become popular through the East.

Directions

(1) First couple bows, swings and leads to the right, and joins the second couple. Standing in a circle, the four dancers each face to their left, and put their right hand on the right shoulder of the person ahead of them. They walk forward in this direction, clockwise. (2) They turn, face in the opposite direction, place left hands on the left shoulder of the person ahead, and walk in a counter-clockwise direction. (3) With his right hand, each dancer reaches across his chest and takes the left hand of the person behind him (Diagram 26). (4) Without letting go, each dancer raises his right hand and does a quarter turn to the right, ducking under his own arm. The dancers are now facing out and circling to the left, hands still joined. (5) The first couple now raises its arms and ducks under the arch formed by the other couple. The boy turns clockwise, and the girl counter-clockwise, "wringing the dishrag," and continuing to hold hands. When the first couple has passed under its own arms, the dancers pull the other couple through. (6) The two girls do a half chain, returning to their partners. (7) The first couple then leads to the third, and then the fourth couple, repeating the action, but omitting the first swing. (8) When each couple has done the action, all the dancers join hands in a large circle of eight, and repeat the entire figure. Each boy ends up with a new partner at this point, but the caller directs each couple in turn, to take the lead in pulling the other couples through. When this has been done four times, with the entire set doing the "wheel," the dancers are back with their original partners.

Calls

(1) First couple bow and swing,
Lead to the right, to the right of the ring.
Up with the right and form a wheel,
(2) Back with the left and grind that meal.
(3) Take that hand upon your shoulder,
(4) Duck right under but still you hold 'er.
(5) Now, first couple, it's up to you,
Raise your arms and pull them through.
(6) Ladies half chain!
(7) *Repeat calls (1) through (6), omitting the first swing.
Each couple leads out in turn.*
(8) Everybody, this time!
Up with the right and form a wheel,
Back with the left and grind that meal.
Take that hand upon your shoulder,
Duck right under but still you hold 'er.
Now, first couple, it's up to you,
Raise your arms and pull them through.

Diagram 26. The Mill Wheel

SASHAY AND SWING THE GIRL BEHIND YOU

Paul Kermiet, director of the Rocky Mountain Folk Dance Camp on Lookout Mountain, Colorado, calls this version of a popular Western square.

Directions
(1) First couple goes to the right and circles to the left with the second couple. (2) All four dancers release hands. The boys take four sliding steps to the right, behind their partners (Diagram 27). At the same time the girls slide four steps to their left, in front of the boys. They all clap hands on the fourth count. (3) They now take four slide steps back on the same track, just the way they came. They clap, and pass right and left through with the opposite couple. As they pass through them, they hold right hands momentarily with the opposite person. (4) Each couple has passed through the opposite couple and is standing back to back with them. Each boy now takes his partner's left hand in his left hand, and bows to her. Releasing hands, the partners turn away from each other (boy turning to his left, girl to her right) to face their opposites. They all swing the opposite person, first boy swinging the second girl, first girl swinging the second boy. (5) Each boy now puts the opposite girl on his right, and has her as his new partner, in repeating the figure with the same couple. The first couple then repeats the entire figure with couples three and four. Each of the other couples then lead out in turn, to do the entire figure.

Calls
(1) First couple out to the right and circle four.
(2) Sashay partners halfway round.
(3) Now re-sashay and pass right through.
(4) Then balance to and swing the girl behind you.
(5) Now circle four and do it again!
Sashay partners halfway round.
Now re-sashay and pass right through.
Then balance to and swing the girl behind you.
(*The first couple repeats calls (1) to (5) with the third and fourth couples in turn.*)

Diagram 27. Sashay and Swing the Girl Behind You

WAGON WHEEL

Here is a popular square from West Texas, as called by the veteran and well-traveled Lone Star caller, Jimmy Clossin.*

Directions

(1) The first couple walks to the right, joins hands with the second couple and circles left. (2) The first boy leaves his partner there, goes on to the third couple and circles left with them. (3) He takes the third girl on to the fourth couple and circles left with them. He leaves the girl there and goes home alone. (4) The side boys lock arms with the girls on either side of them, forming lines of three. These lines of three walk forward and back. The head boys walk forward and back to place. (5) The lines of three walk forward, and wheel around, maintaining a parallel relation to the opposite line. They back into the place of the opposite line of three, thus changing places. (6) The two head boys change places. Everyone has now crossed over. (7) The side boys, who had been between the girls, cross over. They give their right hands to the girl on the right, and walk around her, holding hands high. They give left hands to the girl on the left and walk around her. (8) The side boys take the right hand girl and promenade around the outside of the ring with her. As they do this the two head boys take the other girls and promenade them to the center and back, twice, to get out of the way of the two couples coming around the outside of the ring. (9) The dance is then repeated as before, except that the two end boys join hands as they trade place—and the same for the two side boys. After this, all couples are back with their original partners and ready for a break call, before the second couple begins the figure.

Calls

(1) First couple lead to the right,
Circle four with all your might.

(2) Leave that lady, on to the next, and ring up three.
Steal that lady like honey from a bee.

(3) On to the next and circle four.
Leave that lady and balance home alone.

(4) Side six forward to the center and back to the bar.
End gents forward and back like a shooting star.

(5) Side six swing around as you cross over.

(6) End gents go on to Dover.

(7) Side gents hurry up 'fore it's all over,
All round your right hand lady with your hands up high.
Now the left hand lady like a butterfly.

(8) With right hand lady promenade the ring,
While the roosters crow and the birdies sing.

(9) Side six forward to the center and back to the bar.
End gents forward and back like a shooting star.
Side six swing around as you cross over,
Spread out pretty like a three leaf clover.
End gents down the center with a right hand swing.
Side gents the very same thing.

*Jimmy Clossin, and Carl Hertzog, *West Texas Square Dances,* El Paso, Texas: published by Carl Hertzog, 1948.

THE ROUTE

Definitely not a dance for beginners is this involved square, as called by Ralph Piper, the tireless folk and square dance teacher and caller of the University of Minnesota.

Directions
(1) The first and third couples balance and swing, then promenade to the right, halfway around the outside of the set. (2) The first couple now faces the fourth couple, and the third faces the second. They do a right and left through and a right and left back with the couple they are facing (see page 12). They do a ladies chain and a ladies chain back with the couple they are facing. (3) They then join hands and circle left with that couple. The first circles with the fourth, and the third with the second. Each circle then opens up into a line of four dancers, and the lines face each other, across the set. In each line of four, the active, or head couple, is nearest its home position. (4) The line of four take four steps forward and four steps backward. They then do a right and left through and a right and left back. (5) The girls then do a ladies chain, in which each girl chains completely around the set, moving from boy to boy (Diagram 28). The first and third girls move in a counter-clockwise direction around the set, as they chain. The second and fourth girls move in a clockwise direction. (6) When each girl has returned to her original partner, the lines join hands and circle left again as they did before in (3). The head two couples duck through arches formed by the side two couples, returning to their home positions. There they swing their partners. The dance is then repeated from the beginning with the side two couples leading out to their right, from (1) through (6).

Calls
(1) First and third couples balance and swing,
Promenade halfway round the ring.
(2) Right and left through, right and left back.
Two ladies chain and chain right back.
(3) Circle four and form a line.
(4) Forward eight and fall back eight.
Right and left through, right and left back.
(5) Ladies chain across the line,
Ladies chain down the line,
Ladies chain across the line,
Ladies chain down the line.
(6) Circle four as you did before,
Head two couples duck on o'er,
And everybody swing!

Diagram 28. The Route

SUZIE Q

Originated by caller Jim York of Los Angeles, this fast-moving Western square is contributed by Virginia Anderson.

Directions

(1) The first and third couples balance and swing. They each lead out to the couple on their right and circle four with them. The first couple circles with the second and the third with the fourth. (2) The circles then open into lines of four, facing each other, as in "The Route" (see page 42). In these lines of four, the first and third couples are on the left, nearest their home positions. (3) The lines of four walk forward and back, then forward and pass right and left through. (4) The dancers then do a "Grange Do-Si-Do." Turning, they give right hands to the opposite girl and walk around her. The first boy does this with the fourth girl, the second boy with the third girl, the third boy with the second girl and the fourth boy with the first girl. They then turn their own partners, holding left hands, all the way around. They turn opposite girls, holding right hands, again, and then their own partners, holding left hands. (5) They now turn and form new lines of four, to face *down* and *up* the set. In one line, the first couple is on the left, and couple four on their right, and in the opposite line the third couple is on the left and the second couple on their right. (6) They repeat the action, going forward and back, doing a right and left through, doing the "Grange Do-Si-Do," and then forming new lines *across* the set. The action is repeated twice more, with the lines facing across and down the set, until the dancers are back in their home positions.

Calls

(1) First and third balance and swing,
And lead right out to the right of the ring.
(2) Circle four in the middle of the floor,
And spread out four in a line.
(3) Forward eight and back with you,
Forward again with a right and left through,
(4) And turn right back with a Suzie Q.
Opposite right and a right hand round,
Partner left as she comes down,
Opposite right and right all around,
Partner left and turn her around,
(5) And form new lines of four.
(6) Forward eight and back with you,
Forward again with a right and left through,
And turn right back with a Suzie Q.
Opposite right and a right hand round,
Partner left as she comes down,
Opposite right and right all around,
Partner left and turn her around,
And form new lines of four.

FORWARD SIX AND FALL BACK EIGHT

Here is a Colorado dance, as called by Lloyd Shaw.* When the whole floor of dancers moves in this dance, an exciting rhythmic pattern is created!

Directions

(1) The first couple balances and swings, then walks down the center of the set, and divides the third couple. The first girl turns to her right and takes the hand of the third boy, standing on his left. The first boy turns to his left and stands at the right of the third girl, taking her hand. They form a straight line of four dancers, facing the center of the set. (2) This line takes four steps forward, and four steps back to place. (3) The line then takes four sliding steps to the right until it is directly behind the fourth couple. The first boy and girl take the free hands of the fourth couple, forming a flattened circle of six, all facing the center. (4) These six dancers walk four steps forward (Diagram 29), toward the second couple. As they retire four steps, the second couple, facing them, follows them. (5) All eight dancers now take four steps toward the second couple's position, with the circle of six moving forward, and the second couple walking backward. (6) The second couple now remains in place, as the circle of six retire to place. (7) The original line of four leave the fourth couple and slide four steps to the right, to the position of the first couple. They advance and retire again, and then slide to the right, behind the second couple. Taking their hands, they advance and retire as in (4), (5) and (6). They then slide around to the right, to the third couple's position. They advance and retire again. (8) They join hands in a circle of four in the center of the set. The two girls do a do-si-do around each other, and then the two boys. They join hands again, do a Western *docey-doe* (see page 45), and then the first couple returns to place and all swing.

Calls

(1) First couple balance-swing,
Down the center and split the ring.
The lady goes right and the gent goes left,
And four in line you stand.
(2) Forward four and fall back four,
(3) Sashay four to the right.
(4) Forward six, fall back eight
(5) Forward eight,
(6) Fall back six.
(7) Sashay four to the right.
Forward four and fall back four,
Sashay four to the right.
Forward six, fall back eight.
Forward eight, fall back six.
Sashay four to the right.
Forward four and fall back four.
(8) Forward four and circle four.
Ladies doe and the gents you know.
Circle again and docey-doe.
Balance home and everybody swing.

Diagram 29. Forward Six and Fall Back Eight

*Lloyd Shaw, Cowboy Dances, Caldwell, Idaho: Caxton Printers, Ltd., 1947.

SQUARE DANCES OF TODAY

FOUR IN A CENTER LINE

This Colorado dance, as called by Lloyd Shaw* is similar in formation to "Down The Line," (page 36) but the action of the square is different.

Directions
(1) The first couple balances and swings, then promenades to the right, halfway around the outside of the ring. They stand to the left of the third couple and join hands in a line of four with them. (2) The line takes four steps forward toward the center, and four steps back. It then advances four steps forward, and stands there. (3) Each side couple separates. The side girl walks down the right side of the line of four, as the side boy walks down the left side (Diagram 30). Each boy takes the opposite girl by the right hand and passes her. (4) When the side boys meet their partners at the opposite end of the line, they turn them with a ladies chain turn, in order to face down the line again. The side two couples now separate and return to their home positions again in the same manner, along the sides of the line of four. Returning to their places, they are turned by their partners to face down the line again. (5) The line of four now separates slightly, leaving a gap in the middle. The two side girls advance toward each other, on the right of the line, give each other right hands and pass through the gap (Diagram 31). The opposite side boys turn them with a ladies chain turn, and then they chain back through the line again, and are turned by their partners. (6) The line of four now joins hands in a circle, and does a version of the Western *docey-doe*. Each boy passes his girl's left hand from his right hand to his left, and she passes between the opposite couple in making the change. Each now passes the girl behind him around his left side, lets go her hand, and, still facing the opposite boy, reaches with his right hand for the opposite girl who is now coming around from behind the opposite boy. Each turns the new girl around behind him on his right side and reaches with his left hand for his own partner who has gone around the opposite boy and is now coming from behind him. Each puts his right hand around his own partner's waist and turns her to position.

Calls on next page

Diagram 30. Four in a Center Line

*Lloyd Shaw, *Cowboy Dances*, Caldwell, Idaho: Caxton Printers, Ltd., 1947.

Calls
(1) First couple balance, first couple swing.
    Promenade halfway round the ring.
(2) Four hands in line to the center and back,
    To the center again and there stand pat.
(3) Side couples right and left along the four.
(4) Right and left back as you were before.
(5) Side ladies change through the center of the four,
    And change right back as they were before.
(6) Center four with a circle four.
    Now docey-doe with the gents you know,
    The lady go si and the gent go doe.

Diagram 31. Four in a Center Line

YUCAIPA TWISTER

Contributed by Virginia Anderson, this dance was originated by Ed Gilmore of Yucaipa, California. Its action is typical of many of the dances that have spread over the country, from the West Coast.

Directions
(1) All the dancers do the allemande left with their corners. (2) All the boys then turn their partners with a right forearm turn, with each dancer gripping his partner's forearm with his hand. Each boy then goes into the center of the set. The boys join left hands and do a left hand star, as the girls remain in place. (3) The boys then turn and do a right hand star. When they meet their partners, they catch them with left arms around their waists. (4) They continue to walk around the set in a star promenade, as in "Texas Star" (see page 32). (5) The boys now release right hands and swing out backwards, turning, with their partners, one and a half times. The girls now join left hands in the

center and return to their home positions with a star promenade. (6) The girls now release their partners and continue to do a left hand star. The boys turn and walk, in a clockwise direction, around the set (Diagram 32). (7) Meeting their partners on the opposite side of the set, they turn them with a right forearm turn, once around. (8) They turn the corner girls with a left forearm turn, halfway round. (9) Again they turn partners with a right forearm turn, completely around. (10) They turn the girl on the boy's right with a left forearm turn. (11) They turn partners completely with a right forearm turn. (12) They do an allemande left, grand right and left, meet their partners and swing twice around. (13) They do-si-do corners, turn and meet partners and join right hands. The girls whirl under their joined right hands. The boys then release them, turn to the corner girls, and promenade them to the boys' original home positions. They swing the new partners and repeat the entire figure three more times.

Calls

(1) Go to the left with the old left wing.
(2) A right hand round your own sweet thing,
And star by the left in the center of the ring.
(3) The right hand back and take your pretty maid.
(4) Walk right around in a star promenade.
(5) The gents swing out and the ladies swing in,
Go full around and we're gone again.
(6) The gents double back on the outside track.
(7) You meet your own with the right hand round,
Go all the way around.
(8) Then to the left with the left hand round,
Halfway round.
(9) Back to your own with the right hand round,
Go all the way around.
(10) The right hand lady with the left hand round,
Halfway round,
(11) Your own by the right, go all the way around.

(12) Go to the corner with a left allemande.
You right to your own and a right and left grand.
It's hand over hand around the ring.
When you meet your own you give her a swing.
(13) Do-sa the corner girl, give your own a pretty little whirl,
And all run away with the corner girl.

Diagram 32. Yucaipa Twister

TURKEY IN THE STRAW

SOLDIER'S JOY

LITTLE BROWN JUG

SQUARE DANCES OF TODAY

MISS McLEOD'S REEL

DEVIL'S DREAM

Chapter Five

THE SINGING SQUARES

THE singing square dance call is most popular in the Eastern section of the United States, particularly in the New England states. In many communities in New York, New Jersey, Massachusetts and Connecticut, only singing squares are done.

This was not always the case. Rod La Farge, editor of *Rosin The Bow*, and the organizer of many jamborees and mass square dances in New Jersey, points out that the style of singing the entire call to the melody line has been a development of the past twenty years or so and has become popular with the development of the public address system. La Farge cites as an example the square dances held at the country summer resort owned by an uncle of his during the first World War. At these dances only two or three of all the individual calls were of the singing variety. All of the others were "prompt" calls, in which only the most important directions were spoken, not sung, by the caller.

Today, however, singing calls are becoming increasingly popular throughout the country. If the tunes used are well-known, catchy melodies they help to make the dances more appealing. Often the dancers will sing or hum a familiar section of the call as they dance. In the properly-done singing call, the words and action fit the music exactly; therefore the steps of the dancers must be precisely timed. When this is mastered, it adds considerably to the enjoyment of the dances.

However, it is often difficult to find records in suitable keys and tempi for many of the melodies of the singing calls. Also, because the timing is so precise, if either the caller or the dancers fall behind the music, the sets on the floor may easily become confused and discouraged. For this reason, a singing square must be taught thoroughly and, if it is new to a group, should be walked through at a tempo similar to that of the actual melody.

In this chapter, fifteen singing calls are presented. A number of them are old standby calls—done widely throughout the country. Six have been contributed by outstanding singing callers, as they call them for their own dancers. In calling these dances, the caller need not memorize the language exactly. Instead, he should concentrate on getting the action to synchronize properly with the music, using the original words as far as possible, but adding his own, when he chooses. Often, too, the singing caller will not follow the melody line exactly through the entire call. Instead, in order to emphasize key calls, or to add flavor to the call, he may harmonize with the melody, and even chant sections of the call.

No two callers have exactly the same technique—and it is up to the beginning caller to develop his own, rather than attempt to copy the style of an outstanding caller whom he may happen to admire.

RED RIVER VALLEY

Set to an old folk melody, this dance has many variations. Here is one of the best known versions.

Directions
(1) All the dancers do an allemande left and grand right and left. They meet their partners and all promenade home. (2) The first couple leads out to the second couple, joins hands with them and circles, first to the left and then to the right. (3) Each boy swings the opposite girl and then his own partner. (4) The first couple leads on to the third couple, repeats the action with them, and then with the fourth. Each couple leads out in turn.

Calls
Introduction
(1) Oh, it's allemande left on the corner,
And a grand right and left halfway round.
When you meet with your partner in the valley,
Then you promenade her back home.

Figure
(2) Now the first couple lead down the valley,
Circle four to the left and to the right.
(3) Then you swing with the other fellow's baby,
And you swing with your Red River Girl.
(4) *Repeat (2) and (3) as the first couple goes on to the third and fourth couples.*
Repeat entire dance for each couple in turn.

SQUARE DANCES OF TODAY

RED RIVER VALLEY

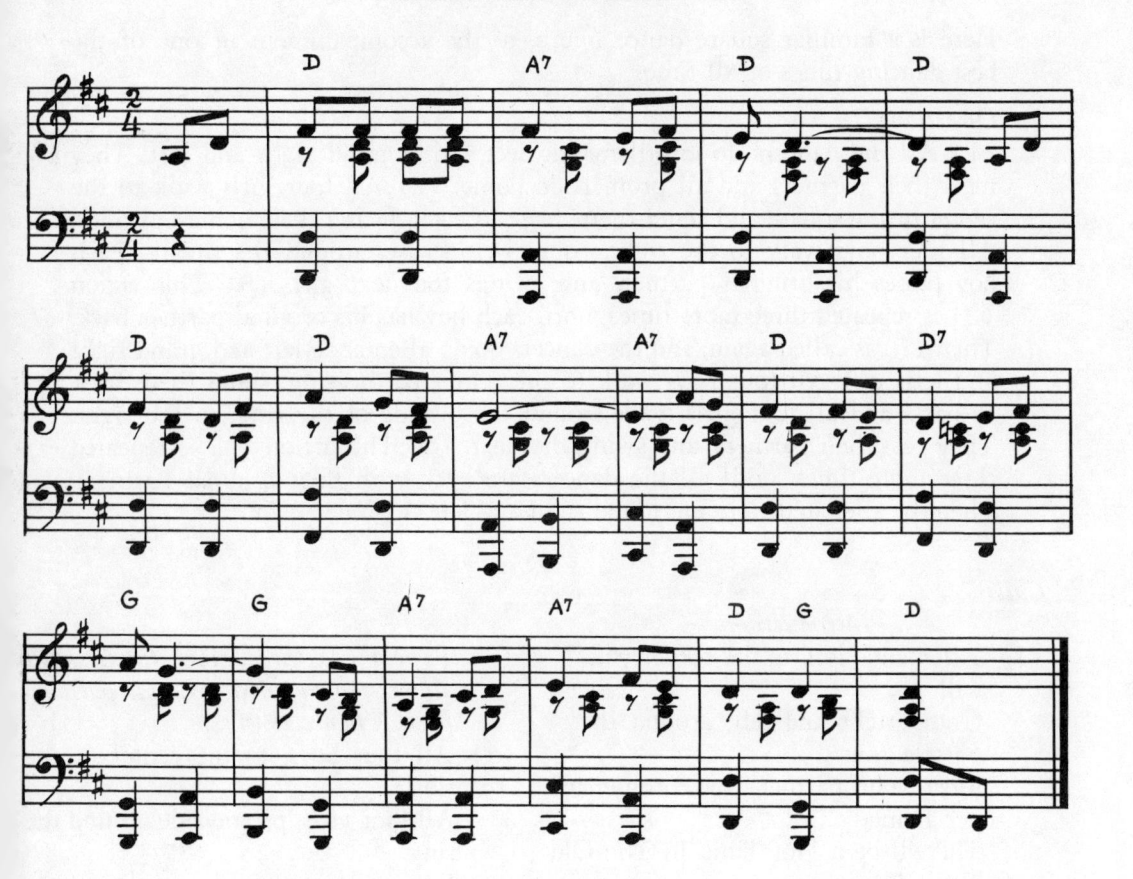

HOT TIME IN THE OLD TOWN

Here is a familiar square dance figure, to the accompaniment of one of the best dancing tunes of all time.

Directions

(1) All the dancers do an allemande left and a grand right and left. They meet their partners and all promenade home. (2) All four girls walk to the center of the square and stand there, back to back, facing their home positions. All four boys walk to the right, counter-clockwise, around the square. Each boy passes his original partner, and swings the next girl. (3) This action (2) is repeated three more times, until each boy has his original partner back. Then (1) is called again, and the dancers do an allemande left and grand right and left. (4) All four boys walk to the center of the ring, stand there back to back, and all four girls walk around the outside of the ring, to the right. They pass their partners, and swing the next. (5) This action (4) is repeated three more times, until all the dancers are back with their original partners. Then the allemande left and grand right and left are done again.

Calls

Introduction

(1) Allemande left, to the corner you will go.
Grand right and left, around the outside row.
Meet your partner, and promenade her home,
There'll be a Hot Time In The Old Town Tonight.

Figure

(2) All four girls, to the center of the ring.
All four boys, promenade around the ring.
Pass your partner, the next one you will swing,
There'll be a Hot Time In The Old Town Tonight.

(3) *Repeat (2) three more times, until all boys have their original partners back. Then call (1).*

(4) All four boys, to the center of the ring,
All four girls, promenade around the ring.
Pass your partner, the next one you will swing,
There'll be a Hot Time In The Old Town Tonight.

(5) *Repeat (4) three more times, until all girls have their original partners back. Then call (1).*

SQUARE DANCES OF TODAY

HOT TIME IN THE OLD TOWN

Copyright Edward B. Marks Music Corporation. Used by permission.

DARLING NELLIE GRAY

Done to a popular song of the last century, this dance vies with "Red River Valley" and "Hot Time In The Old Town" as an all-time favorite singing call.

Directions

(1) All the dancers join hands and circle, first to the left and then back to the right. (2) They do an allemande left and a grand right and left, meet their partners and promenade home. (3) The first couple leads out to the right, joins hands with the second couple, and circles with them, first to the left and then back to the right. All four dancers release hands. The first boy joins right hands with the second girl, and walks past her, passing right shoulders. At the same time, the first girl does the same action with the second boy. Dropping hands, they turn, face the opposite person again, join left hands with that person and walk past each other, passing left shoulders. Releasing hands, they swing their own partners. (4) The first couple leads on and repeats the figure (3) with the third and fourth couples, then goes home for the allemande left and grand right and left (2). Each couple leads out in turn with the same action.

Calls

Introduction

(Music A)
(1) Oh, it's all join hands and you circle to the left,
To the tune of my darling Nellie Gray.
Now you're all going wrong, so go back the other way,
And you circle with your Nellie in the hall.

(Music B)
(2) Now it's allemande left with the lady on the left,
Right hand your partner, grand right and left.
When you meet your partner, then you promenade her home,
Promenade with your darling Nellie Gray.

Figure

(Music A)
(3) Oh, the first couple out to the couple on the right,
You circle to the left, and you circle to the right.
It's a right hand over, and a left hand back,
And you swing with your darling Nellie Gray.

(4) *Repeat (3) twice more. Then call the allemande left (2).*
Then the other couples lead out in turn, to do the figure.

DARLING NELLIE GRAY

HINKEY DINKEY PARLEZ VOUS

This is a good, easily-learned square, with action that appeals readily to beginners.

Directions

(1) All the dancers do an allemande left and a grand right and left. They meet their partners and all promenade. (2) The head two girls take four steps forward, toward each other, and then four steps back to place. The same two girls walk forward, do-si-do, passing around each other back to back, and return to their place. All the dancers do the do-si-do with their corners and then with their partners. (3) They all swing their partners and then promenade once around the set. (4) The side two girls take four steps forward and back, then forward and do-si-do. All the dancers do-si-do their corners and then their partners. (5) All swing partners and promenade around. (6) Repeat the allemande left and grand right and left (1). Then the head two boys do the figure (2) and (3). Then the side two boys do the figure (2) and (3). End the square with the allemande left and grand right and left.

Calls

Introduction

(1) Allemande left your corners all, parlez vous,
Grand chain eight around the hall, two by two.
Meet your partner, what do you do, promenade her two by two,
Hinkey Dinkey Parlez Vous!

Figure

(2) Head two girls go forward and bow, parlez vous,
Same two girls you do-si-do, parlez vous.
Do-si-do your corners all, do-si-do your partners all,
Hinkey Dinkey Parlez Vous!

(3) Swing your partner round and round, parlez vous,
And promenade around the town, parlez vous,
Promenade eight, promenade all, places all and hear my call,
Hinkey Dinkey Parlez Vous!

(4) Side two girls go forward and bow, parlez vous,
Same two girls you do-si-do, parlez vous,
Do-si-do your corners all, do-si-do your partners all,
Hinkey Dinkey Parlez Vous!

(5) Swing your partner round and round, parlez vous,
And promenade around the town, parlez vous.
Promenade eight, promenade all, places all and hear my call,
Hinkey Dinkey Parlez Vous!

(6) *Repeat call (1). Then call (2) and (3) for the head two boys, and (4) and (5) for the side two boys. End with (1) again.*

SQUARE DANCES OF TODAY

HINKEY DINKEY PARLEZ VOUS

UPTOWN AND DOWNTOWN

Sung to the tune of "Golden Slippers," this is a popular square dance throughout most of the East. The action is not difficult, but the boys must be sure to swing their *corner* girls each time, and to take them as their new partners.

Directions

(1) All the dancers do an allemande left and grand right and left, meet their partners and all promenade home. (2) The first couple, holding hands (the girl's left and the boy's right) walks up the set toward the third couple. Joining free hands with them, they walk back down the set with them, toward the first couple's position. They walk back up the set with them again, to the third couple's position. (3) The third couple drops hands and separates, and the first couple walks through them, dividing them. The first girl walks around the outside of the set to the right, returning to her home position, as the first boy walks around to the left. The first couple meets in their home position, with a right elbow swing. (4) All the dancers swing their corner girls, with a regular buzz swing. Then they promenade them around the set to the boys' home positions. (5) The first boy repeats this figure with a new partner. Then the second boy does it *twice*. The third boy does it *twice*. The fourth boy does it *twice*. End with allemande left and grand right and left again.

Calls

Introduction

(Music A)

(1) Oh, it's allemande left to your left hand,
Go right to your own and a right and left grand,
Grand chain eight around the land,
You hurry, hurry round.
Meet your partner, promenade there,
Promenade around the square,
Promenade eight and promenade all,
Places, hear my call!

Figure

(Music A)

(2) First couple up center and away uptown,
Bring that other couple down,
Pick them up and let them fall,
Here you go all around the hall.

(3) Lady go gee and gent go haw,
Right elbow swing as you did before,
Elbow swing as you go round,
And swing your corner lady.

(Music B)

(4) Swing your corner lady, swing her round and round,
Now all promenade, go round the town, promenade around.
Tap your heel and save your toe,
Chicken in the breadpan scratching dough,
Places all and hear my call, ready, here we go!

(5) *The first boy repeats the action from (2) to (4). Each boy in turn does this same action twice. End with (1).*

SQUARE DANCES OF TODAY

GOLDEN SLIPPERS

CAPTAIN JINKS

One of the many dances that go under this name, this singing square involves fast action, in which each boy gets to dance in turn with each of the girls in the set.

Directions

(1) All the dancers do-si-do their corners, then their partners. (2) All the dancers do an allemande left with their corners. Then they do an allemande right with their partners, giving right hands to partners, walking around them, and returning to place. (3) All the dancers face their corners, join right hands with them, and do the step-swing balance with them (see page 11). (4) All the dancers swing their corners, and promenade to the boys' home positions. The entire dance is repeated three more times, each time with new partners and corners, until each boy is back with his original partner.

Calls
(Music A)
(1) Do-si-do your corners all,
   Your corners all, your corners all,
   Do-si-do your partners all,
   For that's the style in the army.
(2) Allemande left your corners all,
   Your corners all, your corners all,
   Allemande right your partners all,
   For that's the style in the army.
(3) Balance to your corners all,
   Your corners all, your corners all,
   Swing your corner lady all,
   And promenade around the hall.

(Music B)
(4) When I left home, mama she cried,
   Mama she cried, mama she cried,
   When I left home, mama she cried,
   He's not cut out for the army!

CAPTAIN JINKS

PASS THE LEFT HAND LADY UNDER

This square has been called to such diverse tunes as "Pistol Packing Mama" and "Devil's Dream." But most often it is called to "Camptown Races," as it is here.

Directions
(1) All the dancers do an allemande left and a grand right and left, meet their partners and promenade home. (2) The first couple walks to the right, joins hands with the second couple and circles left with them. The first boy leaves his partner with the second boy, and goes on alone to the third couple. He circles left with them. He takes the third girl on to the fourth couple, and circles left with them. He leaves the third girl there and returns alone to his home position. (3) The head boys are standing alone; the side boys each have a girl on either side of them, forming lines of three. These lines of three take four steps forward, bow, and four steps back to place. The two head boys walk forward, do-si-do, and return to place. The side boys now raise the left hand of the girl on their right, and pass the left hand girl in front of them, through this arch. At the same time, the right hand girl crosses in front of them (Diagram 33). Each girl crosses in front of the side boy, and goes on to the nearest side of the head boy. (4) Taking the hands of the head boys, they form new lines of three. These lines walk forward and bow, and retire to place. The side boys do-si-do. The girls cross in front of the head boys and walk on to the side boys, taking their hands. (5) Repeat (3). (6) Repeat (4). (7) All swing partners and promenade home. Each couple leads out in turn to do the figure.

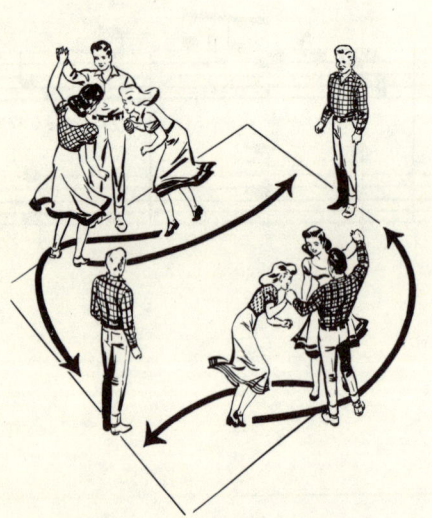

Diagram 33. Pass the Left Hand Lady Under

Calls

Introduction
(Music A)
(1) Allemande left to your left hand,
doo-da, doo-da,
Right to your own and a right and left grand,
Oh, doo-da-day!
Meet your partner, promenade,
doo-da, doo-da,
Promenade eight, promenade all,
Oh, doo-da-day!
(2) First couple out and circle four,
doo-da, doo-da,
Leave that lady, on to the next, circle three hands round.
Take that lady on to the last, doo-da, doo-da,
Leave that lady, home you go,
Oh, doo-da-day!

SQUARE DANCES OF TODAY 67

(Music B)
(3) Forward six and bow, lone gents do-si-do,
    Pass the left hand lady under, Oh, doo-da-day!
(4) Repeat (3)
(5) Repeat (3)
(6) Repeat (3)

(Music A)
(7) Home you go and swing your own, doo-da, doo-da.
    Swing your partner round and round, Oh, doo-da-day.
    Promenade eight and promenade all, doo-da, doo-da,
    Places all and hear my call, Oh, doo-da-day!

CAMPTOWN RACES

DIP AND DIVE

One of the best-looking exhibition figures, done to the tune of "Careless Love," this dance is also one of the most enjoyable for the participants. The author has seen it danced on the main street of a New England village, with one continuous set stretching through more than fifteen squares.

Directions

(1) The first couple walks to the right and joins hands with the second couple. They circle to the left with them, halfway around, so the first couple is on the outside of the set. The first couple now ducks under an arch formed by the second couple, and moves to the center of the set (Diagram 34). Without turning, the first couple raises their hands in an arch, so the fourth couple can duck through. Meanwhile, the second couple turns, so the girl is on the boy's right, and they are facing down the length of the set again. The fourth couple raises an arch for the second couple to duck under. There is a continuous movement, with the first, second and fourth couples doing this dip-and-dive figure, until each couple is back in its home position. (2) The first couple now goes on to the third couple and circles halfway around with them. (3) They duck under an arch formed by the third couple and leave them. They go on to the fourth couple, circle halfway around, and repeat the dip-and-dive figure with the fourth, second and first couples active, until all couples are back in place. (4) All the dancers swing, and promenade home.

Calls

(1) First couple out and circle four,
And you dip and dive across the floor.
Over and under and don't you blunder,
(2) And lead to the next and circle four.
(3) Duck on through and circle four,
And you dip and dive across the floor,

Over and under and don't you blunder,
And home you go and swing your own.
(4) Swing, oh swing your Careless Love,
And you promenade 'neath stars above.
Promenade eight and promenade all,
Promenade your true and Careless Love.

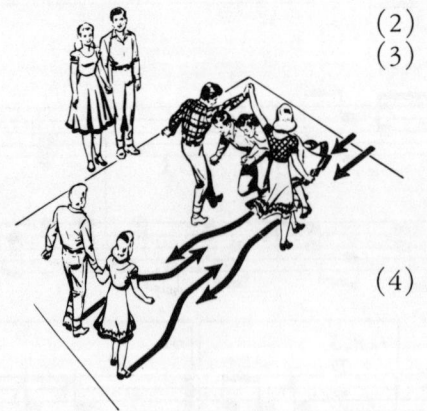

Diagram 34.
Dip and Dive

SQUARE DANCES OF TODAY

CARELESS LOVE

TUCKER'S WALTZ

Here is one that always has the dancers humming it, before it is halfway through. The tune is one that the author learned in the Southwest, under the name of "Tucker's Waltz." The action was first seen in the East.

Directions

(1) The first couple promenades to the right, all the way around the outside of the set. (2) The first girl does a ladies chain with the opposite, or third, girl, and is chained back to place. (3) The first girl does a ladies chain with the girl on her right, the second girl, and then is chained back to place. (4) The first girl does a ladies chain with the girl on her left, the fourth girl, and is chained back to place. (5) All swing and promenade once around the set. (6) The dancers do an allemande left and a grand right and left, meet their partners, and all promenade home. Each couple does the complete figure from (1) in turn.

Calls

Figure

(1) First couple promenade the outside,
Around the outside of the ring.
(2) Two ladies chain, right down the center,
And you chain them back again.
(3) Two ladies chain, the right hand lady,
And you chain them back once more.
(4) Two ladies chain, the left hand lady,
And you chain them home, and everybody swing!

Break

(5) You swing your pretty little baby,
And you promenade around.
You promenade around the set, boys,
And you listen to my call.
(6) Allemande left, upon your corner,
And it's grand chain halfway round.
You meet your partner, and promenade her,
To the tune of Tucker's Waltz!

SQUARE DANCES OF TODAY

TUCKER'S WALTZ

Copyright 1915 by Broadway Music Corporation, copyright renewed 1942 by Broadway Music Corporation. Will Von Tilzer, President, 1619 Broadway, New York, N. Y. Music of foregoing "Tucker's Waltz" was adapted from the music of said copyrighted musical composition "My Little Girl".

TWO HEAD GENTS CROSS OVER

Many different squares are done to the tune of "Life On The Ocean Wave." Here's the way Al Brundage of Stepney, Connecticut, and one of the outstanding callers in the East, calls the figure.

Directions

(1) The two head boys cross the set and swing the opposite girl in her home position. (2) They continue to swing, as the side two boys cross over and do the same thing. (3) All the boys bow to their opposite girls, across the set, then to their new partners, the girls on their right. (4) They then all swing the corner girls, and promenade them once around the set to the girl's original home positions. (5) Every dancer has a new partner. This action (1) through (4) is repeated three more times, until all the dancers have returned to their original partners. (6) The four girls now walk to the center, and join right hands in a star. They walk around to the opposite boy. He swings them. The four girls now join left hands in a star, walk back to partners, and swing their partners. (7) The dance is now repeated from the beginning, with the girls crossing over and doing the action from (1) through (5), and each time promenading to the boy's original position, until they are back with their own partners.

Calls

Figure

(Music A)
(1) The head two gents cross over, and with your opposite swing.
(2) The side two gents cross over, and do the same old thing.
(3) Salute your opposite partner, salute your own sweet Jane.
(4) Swing your corner once around, and promenade the same.

(Music B)
(5) *Repeat calls (1) through (4) three more times.*

Break

(6) Four ladies grand chain, right across you chain.
Swing the opposite gent. Chain the ladies back again.
Trot them back to place. Now everybody swing in place.
(The break call is chanted, and may be called with a "change" tune, or different tune.)

Figure

(7) The head two girls cross over, and with your opposite swing.
The side two girls cross over, and do the same old thing.
Salute your opposite partner, salute your own sweet Jane.
Swing your corner once around, and promenade the same.
Repeat (7) three times more.

SQUARE DANCES OF TODAY

LIFE ON THE OCEAN WAVE

FARMER GRAY

Here is a popular Eastern square, originated by Rod La Farge of New Jersey.*
It is definitely not for those who like their dances sedate and dignified.

Directions

(1) All the dancers throw hands above heads, jump high in the air and give a loud whoop. They all swing partners and promenade once around the set. When they reach their home positions, the boys back up, and swing the girls around in front of them, into place. (2) The first boy leads out, swings the second girl, then takes her home and places her on his partner's left. He steps to his partner's right, and leads the line of three in single file, around the outside of the set to the right (Diagram 35). (3) He repeats (2), adding the third girl to the line. (4) He repeats (2) adding the fourth girl to the line. (5) The four girls now join hands in a circle around the first boy, and circle to the left. *If* they are a young, friendly, boisterous crowd, they then do the action as called; stepping up to the first boy, they muss his hair and tweak his ear, or pull his shirt tail out. *If* they are more reserved, or if the dance is being called in a school class, it is wiser to call "Step right up and spin him around," and to do that action. (6) All then go home and swing partners. Each boy leads out with the figure in turn.

Calls

Introduction

(1) All jump up and give a yell, swing your honey round,
Swing her high and swing her low, promenade the town.

Oh, the farmer, the farmer, the farmer's night in town,
Hey! Hey! Farmer Gray! Swing that gal around.

Diagram 35. Farmer Gray

*Copyright 1948 by Rod La Farge.

Figure

(2) Oh the first gent lead out to the right; swing that girl around.
Take her home and line her up and lead that line around.
Oh, the farmer, the farmer, took another girl away,
Hey! Hey! Farmer Gray! Took another girl away.

(3) Now on to the next and take a swing, swing her up and down.
Take her home and line her up, single file around.
Oh, the farmer, the farmer, took another gal away,
Hey! Hey! Farmer Gray! With his whiskers full of hay!

(4) On to the last and swing that girl, swing her high and low.
Take her home and line her up; around the set you go.
Oh, the farmer, the farmer, took another girl away,
Hey! Hey! Farmer Gray! It's the farmer's turn to pay!

(5) Now the gent stand in the center ring, the ladies circle about.
Step right up and muss his hair, pull his shirt tail out.

(6) Oh, you swing her, you swing her, swing her round and round,
Hey! Hey! Farmer Gray! The farmer's night in town!

FARMER GRAY

The lyrics and music of the composition "Farmer Gray" are based upon the musical composition "The Farmer Took Another Load Away, Hay, Hay" by Edgar Leslie, Charles D. O'Flynn and Larry Vincent, copyright 1925 Clark and Leslie Songs, Inc., copyright assigned 1932 to Edgar Leslie, Inc., 1595 Broadway, New York, N. Y.

LUCY LONG

Paul Hunt, one of the most popular callers in the East, has put this square to an old tune, and it has become a favorite of his Long Island dancers.

Directions

(1) The two head couples walk to the right and circle half around with the side couples. The head couples do a right and left through the sides, walking into the center of the set. (2) They meet the other head couple there. Each head boy swings the opposite girl. Meanwhile the sides turn around to place. (3) Now each head boy takes the girl he was swinging over to the side couple on the boy's right (first girl takes the third girl to couple two). They form a left hand star with that couple. (4) The boys reach their own right hand back over their left shoulders and take the right hand of the girl behind them. They keep circling. As they near the boys' home positions, they drop left hands, pull the girl behind them across and in front of them to their right side. Then they swing with that girl, moving as they swing, back to the boys' home positions. (5) They finish the swing with that girl on their right sides. They allemande left with the next girl on the left, and promenade with the girls they had just been swinging. When the figure is completed, each girl has moved one place to the left. (6) Repeat the action again with the head two couples leading out. Then repeat it twice more with the side couples leading to their right.

Calls

Introduction

(1) Join your hands and circle left, you circle left around.
The other way back on the same old track, you circle right around.
Swing with Miss Lucy, you swing and have some fun.
Allemande left with the corner, promenade the one you swung.

Figure

(2) The two head couples lead to the right and circle half a mile,
Pass right through the other two and swing the opposite gal.
Swing with Miss Lucy, oh, swing where you are,

(3) Take that lady back to the sides and form a left hand star.

(4) Right hand back to the corner and keep on going strong,
Pull her through with a Whoop-Te-Do and swing Miss Lucy Long.

(5) Swing with Miss Lucy, you swing her all day long.
Allemande left with the corner, promenade the one you swung.

(6) *Repeat (2) through (5) again with the head couples leading out, and then twice more for the side couples leading out.*

SQUARE DANCES OF TODAY

LUCY LONG

WHEN THE WORK'S ALL DONE THIS FALL

Here's the figure to one of Lawrence Loy's favorite calls—and it means fast stepping for the dancers!

Directions

(1) The first couple leads to the right and circles four hands to the left with the second couple. The first boy leaves his girl there and goes on to circle three to the left with the third couple. He takes the third girl with him to the fourth couple, and circles left with them. He leaves the third girl there and goes to his home position alone. (2) The side two boys each have their partner on their right, and another girl on their left. The side boys join right hands with the girl on their right and walk around her. The side boys join left hands with the girl on their left and walk around her. (3) The side boys, with the girl on their right, walk forward and do a right and left through with the couple across the way (Diagram 36). They turn and do a right and left back. (4) They join both hands with the girl on their left and sashay across the floor, taking eight slide steps across and eight slide steps coming back. As they cross, the boys pass back to back, and as they return, the girls pass back to back. (5) The head two boys now walk forward and do-si-do. (6) All the dancers do an allemande left and promenade their partners to their home positions. Each couple then repeats the figure in turn, from (1) through (6).

Diagram 36. When the Work's All Done This Fall

SQUARE DANCES OF TODAY

Calls

Figure

(1) The first old couple go to the right and circle four hands round.
Leave the lady, go to the next and circle three hands round.
Take that lady to the last and circle four hands round.
Say goodbye and leave her there and go to your stamping ground.

(2) The two side gents turn the right hand lady
With the right hand right around.
Now turn the left hand lady with the left hand once around.

(3) With the right hand lady you right and left with the couple over there, Now right and left right back again, for they're a jolly pair.

(4) With the left hand girl you now sashay with the couple cross the way.
Now sashay right back again, you haven't long to stay!

(5) The lonesome gents they do-si-do around on heel and toe.

(6) Now allemande left your corner, take your own and away you go.
Promenade your partner, just once around the room.
The next old couple starts to dance, when I begin the tune.

WHEN THE WORK'S ALL DONE THIS FALL

HOT TIME IN THE OLD TOWN

Here's another call to the tune of "There'll Be A Hot Time In The Old Town Tonight." (Music on page 57.) It has been travelling around the country and has caught on in many sections. This is the way Earl Brooks of Delaware calls the dance.

Directions

(1) The first couple leads to the second couple, joins hands with them, and circles to the left with them. The first boy releases the second girl's hand, and, as they continue to circle, he adds the third couple to the circle. The six dancers circle left, and then the first boy adds two more, adding the fourth couple to the circle. All eight dancers are now circling left. (2) All the boys do an allemande left with their corners. (3) Releasing the corner's hand, each boy walks past his partner, passing right shoulders, but *not* touching her. He does an allemande right with the girl on his right (for the first boy, this would be the second girl), joining right hands with her and walking completely around her. Releasing her hand, he walks back past his partner again, passing left shoulders, and *not* touching her. (4) Each boy does an allemande left with his corner again. Giving his right hand to his partner, each boy walks into a grand right and left. (5) Each boy meets his partner on the other side of the square, does a do-si-do with her, and swings her once or twice around. Then he promenades her back to place. (6) Each couple leads out in turn with the figure (1), and then the action (2) through (6) is repeated.

Calls

Figure

(1) First couple out and circle four hands round.
On to the next and circle six hands round.
On to the next and circle eight hands round,
There'll be a Hot Time In The Old Town Tonight!

Break

(2) Allemande left with the lady on the left.
(3) Allemande right with the lady on the right.
(4) Allemande left with the lady on the left,
And a grand right and left halfway round!
(5) Meet your partner with a do-si-do!
Swing her around, and round and round you go.
And then you promenade the sweetest girl in town,
There'll be a Hot Time In The Old Town Tonight!

RED RIVER VALLEY

Ralph Page of New Hampshire, nationally known caller and dance authority, calls this version of "Red River Valley." (Music on page 55.)

Directions

(1) The first couple walks to the second couple, and faces them. Both couples do the step-swing balance *once,* stepping on their right feet and swinging their left feet across, then stepping on their left feet and swinging the right feet across. (2) The same two couples join hands and circle left one time around, until the first couple is back in the center of the set, facing the second couple. (3) The first, second and fourth couples now do a right and left through, passing through the opposite couple and moving to the end of the set. When they reach the end, they turn around to face the set again, with the girl on the right of the boy. All three couples move simultaneously until they are back in their home positions (Diagram 37). (4) The first couple turns, faces the fourth couple, and does the step-swing balance with them. They then circle once around to the left with them. (5) They now do a dip-and-dive figure (Page 68), with the first couple raising an arch, and the fourth couple ducking under. The fourth couple then raises the arch, and the second couple ducks under. All three couples move, alternating ducking under and raising the arch, until they have returned to their home positions. (6) The second couple now repeats the entire figure, from (1) through (5), dancing with the third and first couples. (7) The head two couples each walk to the side couple on their right, do the step-swing balance with them, circle around, and do a right-and-left-eight figure, with all *four* couples, until they have all returned to place. (8) The third and fourth couples then each lead out, doing the action from (1) through (5) in turn. (9) All the dancers bow to their partners, then corners, then their opposites. Then they all swing their partners.

Calls

Figure

(1) First couple to the right and you balance,
(2) Circle four hands all around you go.
(3) Then you right and left six down the valley,
And you right and left six right back home.
(4) First couple to the left and you balance,
Circle four hands all around you go.
(5) Then you dip and dive six down their valley,
And you dip and dive six to your home.

Diagram 37. Red River Valley (*Calls continued on next page*)

(6) *Second couple repeats (1) through (5)*

(7) The head two couples to the right and balance.
Then you right and left eight in a line.
You right and left in time, you take your steps in time,
You right and left home to your place.

(8) *Third and fourth couples lead out in turn with (1) through (5).*

(9) Address your partners. Honor corners all.
Now bow to the one across the hall.
Swing your partners one and all,
Kiss her quick, or not at all.
(This last verse is chanted, and does not fit the music exactly.)

Chapter Six

CIRCLE AND LONGWAYS DANCES

THE dances presented in Chapters Four and Five were all in the square, or quadrille formation. But the program of a typical square dance session held anywhere in the United States might include a variety of other dances, depending on the locality and the background of the dancers. Among these other dances might be rounds, play parties, and longways.

The term "round dances" applies in general to couple dances, either the modern American foxtrot, or such folk dances as the waltz, polka, schottische or hambo. In many communities there is a custom of alternating three squares with several foxtrots or slow waltzes. In other sections, the more vigorous couple dances might be done instead of these.

The term "play parties" includes the circle and longways singing games, whose history is given on page 1. Easily learned, they are rhythmic, attractive to every age level, and extremely valuable as mixers. In addition to their value in helping the leader introduce many of the square dance steps and movments, they often offer an opportunity for dancing under the most informal conditions. Lynn Rohrbough, of the Cooperative Recreation Service in Delaware, Ohio, has this to say about the use of play parties: " . . . the swing and promenade were traditionally done with the hand position, and the tunes were sung without other musical accompaniment, and thus were useful where there were no instruments of any kind."

He goes on to describe " . . . the types of dancing which can be done on a station platform while people are waiting for a train; at cross roads on hikes, which was the old custom in Ireland; during the ten minute intervals between classes as sometimes happens in Scandinavian folk schools. In America there is surely more need of the spontaneous and informal in this age of over-emphasis on equipment and special leaders."*

The following chapter includes directions, music and singing calls for fourteen circle play parties, couple dances and mixers, and longways. In Chapter Nine, various ways will be outlined in which each of these dances can be worked into square dance sessions for different types of classes and groups. Useful records for these dances are listed on pages 128-129.

* Letter to the author, November 10, 1949.

SHOO FLY

Here is a simple circle play party, ideal for getting a new group into the swing of things!

Formation
A circle of partners with hands joined, all facing the center. Each girl is on her partner's right.

Directions
(1) Keeping hands joined, all take four steps forward, into the center. (2) All take four steps out again, still facing the center. (3) Take four steps in again. (4) Take four steps out. (5) All swing partners, using a two-hand, walk-around swing. (6) Each boy now holds his partner's right hand in his left hand, and turns her in front of him, so she crosses from his right side to his left. (7) All face the center again, and join hands. The boy's former partner is now on his left. The girl who is now on his right is his new partner. The dance is repeated as many times as desired.

Singing Call
(1) Shoo fly, don't bother me
(2) Shoo fly, don't bother me
(3) Shoo fly, don't bother me
(4) 'Cause I belong to somebody
(5) I do, I do, I do
   And I ain't going to tell you who
(6) I belong to somebody
(7) Yes indeed I do

SQUARE DANCES OF TODAY

SHOO FLY

SKATING AWAY

This lively circle dance, requiring no partners, is useful in introducing a circle left and right, a two-handed swing, and a star.

Formation
A circle of dancers with hands joined, face the center. No partners are needed, except for two couples who are in the center of the circle to begin the dance (Diagram 38).

Directions
(1) The circle of dancers, with hands joined, walk to the right, in a counterclockwise direction. As they do this, the four in the center join their right hands in a right-hand-star, and walk in the direction they are facing. (2) The circle now reverses direction, circling clockwise, as the four in the center put their left hands in, and walk in a left-hand-star. (3) Each person in the center chooses a person from the outer circle, and, swinging around with both hands joined, brings this person into the center. Each boy chooses a girl, and each girl a boy. The other dancers clap in rhythm, as they do this. (4) The four who were in the center at the beginning now step into the outside circle, and join hands with them. The new four dancers join hands in a right-hand-star, and are ready to start the play party from the beginning. It is repeated as many times as desired.

Diagram 38. Skating Away

SQUARE DANCES OF TODAY

Singing Call

(1) There were two couples skating away
Skating away, skating away
There were two couples skating away
So early in the morning
(2) The ice was thin, they all fell in
They all fell in, they all fell in

The ice was thin, they all fell in
So early in the morning
(3) The old swing out, the new swing in
The new swing in, the new swing in
The old swing out, the new swing in
(4) So early in the morning

SKATING AWAY

OH SUSANNAH

Always a popular favorite, this play party makes use of the grand right and left. In planning his program, the caller will probably want to put "Oh Susannah" near the beginning, to familiarize his dancers with that call.

Formation
Single circle of couples, with each girl on her partner's right, all facing the center.

Directions
(1) All the girls walk four steps forward into the center, and four steps back out to place. (2) All the boys do the same. (3) All face partners. Give right hand to partners and do the grand right and left, boys going counter-clockwise, and girls clockwise. (4) Counting the original partner as number one, each boy takes the seventh girl he meets as his new partner. He meets this girl on the words "Susannah, don't you cry." Each couple joins hands in skating position, and promenades around the circle in a counter-clockwise direction. If any boy or girl does not find a partner immediately, he or she must step into the center of the circle, hand raised, to find one. (5) All dancers step into the circle again, facing the center, with the girl on her new partner's right. Repeat the dance as often as desired.

Singing Call
(1) I come from Alabama with my banjo
    on my knee
(2) I'm going to Louisiana, my true love
    for to see
(3) It rained all night, the day I left
    The weather it was dry
    The sun so hot, I froze to death
    Susannah, don't you cry
(4) Oh, Susannah, don't you cry for me
    For I'm going to Louisiana
(5) With my banjo on my knee

SQUARE DANCES OF TODAY

OH SUSANNAH

COME MY LOVE

Another lively play party that all can do—young or old. Here is one that usually provokes some robust singing!

Formation
A circle of couples, facing in a counter-clockwise direction, ready to promenade. Boys are on the inside, girls on their right (Diagram 39).

Directions
(1) With hands joined in skating position, all the dancers promenade around, counter-clockwise. (2) All the dancers drop hands. The line of girls continue marching to the right, counter-clockwise. The boys turn about, reversing their direction, and march in a clockwise direction, just inside the circle of girls. (3) On the words, "You're old enough," all take new partners and, joining both hands, swing around in place. Then resume promenade position, and repeat from the beginning, as often as desired, each time with new partners.

Diagram 39. Come My Love

SQUARE DANCES OF TODAY

Singing Call

(1) Come my love and go with me
   Come my love and go with me
   Come my love and go with me
   And I will take good care of thee
(2) You are too young, you are not fit
   You are too young, you are not fit
   You are too young, you are not fit
   You cannot leave your mother yet
(3) You're old enough, you're just about right
   You're old enough, you're just about right
   You're old enough, you're just about right
   I asked your mother last Saturday night

COME MY LOVE

BINGO

Originally an old Welsh-English song, "Bingo" has become one of the best-known play parties of the Southern Highlands. But this particular version happens to hail from much farther West, it is the way boy and girl members of the Farmers Union do the dance in the Black Hills of Dakota!

Formation
Couples, with hands joined in promenade position, facing counter-clockwise in a circle.

Directions
(1) Beginning on their left feet, all the couples march around the circle in a counter-clockwise direction. (2) All the couples now step back into a single circle, join hands, and slide to their right. (3) On the spoken part, partners turn to face each other. They take their partner's hand on the letter "B," and continue with a grand right and left in the direction they are facing. A new person is passed for each letter: "I," "N," and "G." On the final "OHHH!" they hug and whirl the new partner around. If this is not suited to the group, they can simply do a buzz swing with the new partner. Take promenade position with this new partner, and start the dance from the beginning, repeating it as often as desired.

Singing Call
(1) A farmer's black dog
    Sat on the back porch
    And Bingo was his name
    A farmer's black dog
    Sat on the back porch
    And Bingo was his name
(2) B,I,N,G,O, B,I,N,G,O, B,I,N,G,O,
    And Bingo was his name
(3) (Spoken) B, I, N, G, OHHH!
    And Bingo was his name!

BINGO

CHESTER SCHOTTISCHE

Here is a circle mixer done in groups of three—with one girl and two boys, or two boys and one girl dancing together. It is especially useful in a group where the sexes are unevenly distributed. It may be done to any good schottische tune.

Formation
Sets of three, holding hands and facing around the floor in a counter-clockwise direction. The odd boy or girl is between the other two (Diagram 40).

Directions
(1) All the dancers touch their left feet to the floor twice.
(2) All the dancers take three walking steps forward, moving diagonally to the left, leading with the left foot.
(3) All the dancers touch their right feet to the floor twice.
(4) All take three walking steps forward and diagonally to the right, leading with the right foot.
(5) The next step is a complete schottische forward, moving around the circle. All the dancers face forward, and, leading with their left feet, walk three steps forward: left, right, left.
(6) Then, hopping on their left feet, and swinging their right feet forward, they take three more walking steps forward: right, left, right.
(7) Four step-hops, continuing to move forward.
   All the dancers step on their left feet, and hop on the same foot.
   Step on right, and hop on it.
   Step on left and hop on it.
   Step on right and hop on it.

The dance is repeated from the beginning as many times as desired. After the dancers have become thoroughly familiar with the steps, the dance should be taught so that the center dancer (the middle one) advances to the next group each time, moving forward on the four step hops (7).

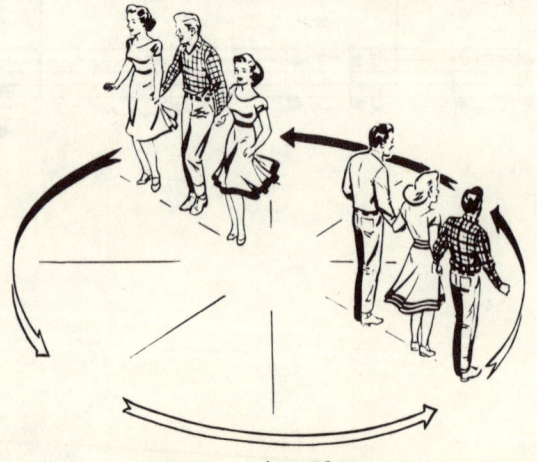

Diagram 40. Chester Schottische

SQUARE DANCES OF TODAY

Prompt Call To Help Dancers
(1) Left AND left, and walk, two, three.
(3) Right AND right, and walk, two, three.
(5) One, two, three HOP, one two, three, HOP.
(7) Step-hop, step-hop, step-hop, step-hop.

CHESTER SCHOTTISCHE

PATTYCAKE POLKA

Here is a lively circle mixer, done to the tune of "Buffalo Gals." Its rollicking rhythm and quick changing of partners make it a favorite everywhere.

Formation

A double circle of partners facing each other. Girls are on the outside, facing toward the center. Boys are on the inside, facing out. They hold each other in regular dance position (Diagram 41).

Directions

(1) The first step is a heel-and-toe, familiar to all folk dancers.
The girl extends her right foot to her right, heel on the ground, toe pointing up. At the same time, the boy extends his left foot to the left, heel on floor, toe pointing up (Diagram 42—left).

(2) She now brings her right foot back, so the toe touches the floor directly in front of her right foot. The boy simultaneously brings his left foot back, so the toe touches the floor in front of his right foot. (Diagram 42—right). This is all done to the first measure, with a springing step.

(3) Repeat (1).

(4) Repeat (2).

(5) All the couples take four sliding steps to the girl's right, and the boy's left. The circle moves around the floor in unison.

(6) Steps one through five are repeated, in exactly the opposite direction. The girl does the heel-and-toe twice, leading with her left foot, as the boy does it with his right foot.
They slide four steps to the girl's left, and the boy's right.

(7) All face partners, dropping hands.
Each boy claps his right hand against his partner's right hand three times.

(8) They clap left hands three times.

(9) They clap both hands against each other three times.

(10) Bending knees slightly, they slap their own knees three times.

(11) All the dancers link right elbows with their partners and walk once around each other, in a clockwise direction.
Leaving their partners, each boy now moves one girl to the left. He takes this girl for his new partner, and begins the dance with her.

Diagram 41. Pattycake Polka

SQUARE DANCES OF TODAY

In teaching the "Pattycake Polka," it is helpful for the caller to call out the action the first few times the dancers do it. Once they become familiar with it, he need no longer do this.

Prompt Call To Help Dancers
- (1) HEEL and TOE, HEEL and TOE
- (5) Slide, slide, slide, slide
- (6) HEEL and TOE, HEEL and TOE
  Slide, slide, slide, slide
- (7) Right, right, right
- (8) Left, left, left
- (9) Both, both, both
- (10) Knees, knees, knees
- (11) Right elbow round and
  Go on to the next

Diagram 42. Pattycake Polka

BUFFALO GALS

THE MEXICAN WALTZ

Everyone knows the catchy Mexican melody, "Chiapanecas." The dance done to it is not Mexican but hails from the Southwestern part of the United States.

Formation

Couples facing around the circle in a counter-clockwise direction. Partners hold inside hands—the girl's left in the boy's right.

Directions

(1) The boy steps to the left with his left foot, swinging his right foot across, as the girl steps to her right, swinging her left foot across (Diagram 43—left).

(2) The boy steps to the right with his right foot, swinging his left foot across, as the girl steps to her left, swinging her right foot across (Diagram 43—right).

(3) The boy places his right foot down next to his left foot with a slight stamp, as the girl places her left foot down next to her right. Release partner's hand.

(4) Each dancer claps his own hands twice.

(5) All turn toward partners, and join the other hand. The boy's left now holds the girl's right. Part (1) is repeated, but everything is now done in the opposite direction. The boy steps to his right, and the girl to her left, swinging the other foot across.

(6) Boy steps to his left, and girl to her right, swinging the other foot across.

(7) The boy places his left foot next to his right, as the girl places her right foot next to her left.

(8) All clap hands twice.

(9) All the dancers face partners, and join both hands with them. They take a balance step apart (Diagram 44—left),

Diagram 43. Mexican Waltz

then together and apart. All clap hands twice.

(10) Joining hands again, they take a balance step together, apart, and then together. They clap hands twice, with their hands around their partner's back (Diagram 44—right).

(11) Waltz with partner for the remainder of the music. The dance is repeated as many times as desired.

Diagram 44. Mexican Waltz

SQUARE DANCES OF TODAY

MEXICAN WALTZ

SICILIAN CIRCLE

Originally an old New England circle dance, "Sicilian Circle" provides a good opportunity to drill the dancers in the *ladies chain* and *right and left through*. It also makes the dancers listen carefully to the music, as everything is done in counts of eight steps. This is a progressive dance, in that each couple goes on to dance with the other couples in the circle.

Formation

Couples standing around the floor in a circle, each girl on her partner's right. Each couple is facing another couple (Diagram 45).

Directions

(1) All the dancers, holding their partner's hands, take four steps toward the opposite couple, bowing slightly on the fourth step. Then they take four steps back to place, without turning. The step throughout is a light, graceful movement.

(2) All the couples walk forward toward the opposite couples, join hands with them, and circle once completely to the left, returning to home positions. It takes eight steps to do this entire figure.

(3) Each couple does a ladies chain with the opposite couple.
   The ladies are chained back to their partners (see page 11).

(4) Each couple does a right and left through with the opposite couple, and a right and left back to place.
   Turn to face the couple again (see page 12).

Diagram 45. Sicilian Circle

SQUARE DANCES OF TODAY

(5) All take four steps forward, and four steps back, as in (1).
(6) All drop hands and walk forward, each couple doing a *pass through* with the opposite couple. The dancers do not turn, but walk straight through and face a new couple in the circle, ready to do the dance from the beginning with them.

The dance is repeated as many times as desired.

SICILIAN CIRCLE

THE NOBLE DUKE OF YORK

Originally a children's game, this play party, done to a familiar tune, is suitable for all ages.

Formation

Longways set of from four to eight couples, in facing lines (Diagram 46). The head couple is the couple nearest the music, and foot couple is the couple farthest away.

Directions

(1) The first couple joins inside hands, the girl's right in the boy's left, and walk eight steps down toward the foot of the set. (2) They turn toward each other, join the other hands, and walk eight steps back up to the head of the set. (3) The first couple joins both hands and does a skipping, turning swing down the length of the set to the foot. (4) The first couple, standing at the foot, now joins hands in an arch. As they do this, the second girl, now the head girl, leads her line to the right, and down the outside of the set to the foot. Simultaneously, the new head boy leads the boys to the left, down the outside to the foot of the set. This is called *cast off*. As the dancers meet their partners, they join hands and go up under the arch formed by the first couple. They go up the line to their places, and step back to form the set again. Every couple has moved up one position, except the first, which is now in the foot position. Repeat the dance once for each couple.

Diagram 46. Longways Formation

SQUARE DANCES OF TODAY

Singing Call
(1) Oh, the noble Duke of York
    He had ten thousand men
(2) He marched them up to the top of the hill
    And he marched them down again
(3) Oh, when you're up you're up
    And when you're down you're down
    And when you're only halfway up
    You're neither up nor down
(4) Oh, a-hunting we will go
    A-hunting we will go
    We'll catch a fox and put him in a box
    And never let him go

THE NOBLE DUKE OF YORK

BOW BELINDA

This is one of the best-known and most enjoyable of the longways dances. It is a good idea to teach "Bow Belinda" and the following dance, "Alabama Girl," to a new group before teaching them the "Virginia Reel," as the dancers will learn most of the steps of the "Virginia Reel" in the first two play parties.

Formation
Lines of four to eight couples facing each other; girls on one side, boys on the other. The head couple is the couple nearest the music, and foot couple is the couple farthest away.

Directions
(1) The first girl and the foot boy, diagonally opposite each other, take four steps toward each other, bow, and four steps back to place (Diagram 47). (2) The first boy and the foot girl do the same. (3) The first girl and last boy walk toward each other, give right hands to each other, walk around each other, and return to place. (4) The first boy and the foot girl do the same. (5) The first girl and the foot boy walk around each other, holding left hands. (6) The first boy and foot girl do the same. (7) The first girl and last boy walk around each other, holding both hands. (8) The first boy and the last girl do the same. (9) The first girl and the last boy do the do-si-do, going around each other, passing right shoulders as they go forward, and left shoulders as they go back. (10) The first boy and the last girl do the same. (11) All join hands with partners, and promenade to the left, and down to the foot of the set, following the first couple. (12) When they are down at the foot, the first boy moves the girl over to her side, and the first couple forms an arch. The other couples go through, as in "The Noble Duke Of York," with only the first couple forming the arch. The lines are formed again, with the head couple now down at the foot. The play party is repeated one time for each couple.

Diagram 47. Bow Belinda

SQUARE DANCES OF TODAY

Singing Call

(1) Bow, bow, bow Belinda, Bow, bow, bow Belinda
(2) Bow, bow, bow Belinda, Won't you be my darling
(3) Right hand round, Oh Belinda, Right hand round, Oh Belinda
(4) Right hand round, Oh Belinda, Won't you be my darling
(5) Left hand round, Oh Belinda, Left hand round, Oh Belinda
(6) Left hand round, Oh Belinda, Won't you be my darling
(7) Two hands round, Oh Belinda Two hands round, Oh Belinda
(8) Two hands round, Oh Belinda Won't you be my darling
(9) Do-si-do, Oh Belinda Do-si-do, Oh Belinda
(10) Do-si-do, Oh Belinda Won't you be my darling
(11) Promenade all, Oh Belinda Promenade all, Oh Belinda Promenade all, Oh Belinda Won't you be my darling
(12) Promenade all, Oh Belinda Promenade all, Oh Belinda Promenade all, Oh Belinda Won't you be my darling

BOW BELINDA

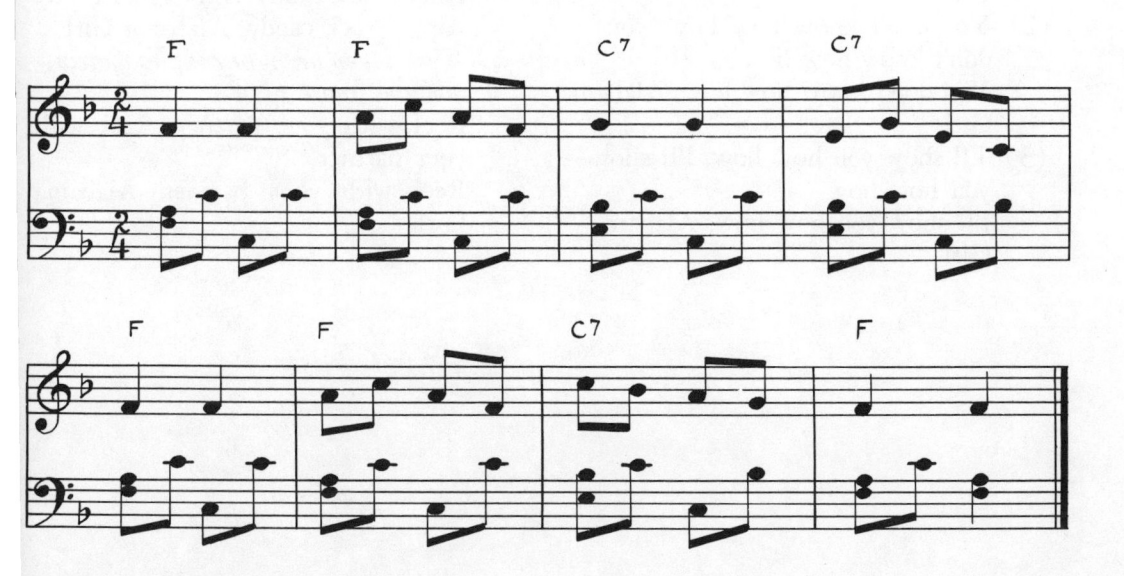

ALABAMA GIRL

There are just two parts to this fast-moving dance. It is a good one to teach a beginner's group, as they can concentrate on learning the reel in it, and not have to worry about other involved steps.

Formation
Longways formation with from four to eight couples.

Directions
(1) The first couple joins hands and walks down the length of the set, eight steps, and walks back eight steps. (2) They then do the reel down the length of the set. To do this, the first couple joins right hands in the center and walks around each other, one and a half times. (3) They then release each other's hands. The boy is facing the girl who is now at the head of the girl's line. He gives his left hand to her and they walk around each other in four counter-clockwise steps. At the same time, the first girl faces the boy who is now at the head of the boy's line. They join left hands and walk around each other in four counter-clockwise steps. The first couple meets in the center again, and turns with a right-hand-round. They then go to the next person in the line with a left-hand-round. They continue down the set in this way, reeling. Each time, the active couple turns in the center with a right-hand-round and goes to the side with a left-hand-round. When they reach the foot of the set, the boy puts the girl in place at the foot of her line, and goes back to the foot of his line. The dance is repeated once for each couple.

Singing Call
(1) Coming through in a hurry, coming through in a hurry
Coming through in a hurry, Alabama Girl
(2) You don't know how how, you don't know how how
You don't know how how, Alabama Girl
(3) I'll show you how how, I'll show you how how
I'll show you how how, Alabama Girl

With five or six couples dancing, add the next verse, to give them time to complete the reel.
Ain't I rock candy, Ain't I rock candy
Ain't I rock candy, Alabama Girl
With seven or eight couples dancing, add one more verse.
Reel with your partner, Reel with your partner
Reel with your partner, Alabama Girl

ALABAMA GIRL

VIRGINIA REEL

Originally this was an English dance, known as "Sir Roger De Coverley." However, it has been done in the United States for so long that it is probably the best-liked of all American country dances. This is the "family-style" version of the "Virginia Reel."

Formation

Longways sets of from four to eight couples. Six couples is the ideal number for this dance.

Directions

(1) All take four steps forward, bow to partner, and four steps back to place. (2) All walk forward, give right hands to partners, walk around partners and back to place. (3) Do the same, joining left hands. (4) Do the same, joining both hands, and turning in a clockwise direction. (5) All do-si-do partners, returning to place. (6) First couple joins both hands with each other, and slides eight steps down the center of the set, and eight steps back to place. (7) First couple now does the reel, as described in "Alabama Girl," page 106. (8) When the first couple reaches the foot of the set, they slide back up to the top again. (9) There they separate, girl going to the head of her line, boy to the head of his. They all face forward, toward the music. (10) At the command "Cast off!" they separate, girls going to the right and down to the foot, and boys to the left, and down to the foot. (11) The first couple forms an arch at the foot, and the others go through it, moving up the set, and forming their lines again. The first couple remains at the foot, and the others have all moved up one position. The dance is repeated once for each couple.

Patter Call (Not to be sung)
(1) Forward and bow to your partners all
(2) Right hand 'round, around the hall
(3) Left hand back and don't be slack
(4) Two hands round and around you go
(5) And now your partners do-si-do
(6) First couple sashay down the set
Sashay back
(7) First couple reel down the set
(8) Get to the foot and sashay back
(9) Form your lines
(10) Cast off!
Girls to the right, boys to the left
(11) Form your lines and all go through
Ready all—from the beginning!

SQUARE DANCES OF TODAY 109

IRISH WASHERWOMAN

THE GRAND MARCH

At square dances all over the country, the "Grand March" is a time-honored institution. It may go under a variety of different names and may employ a variety of patterns, but it is always good fun and an ideal way to have the dancers mix with each other. It is usually easy to get a crowd of dancers into a "Grand March"—because all they have to do is walk. If they can walk there is no reason for their sitting.

Formation

A good way to begin the "Grand March" is to form two parallel lines, one of girls and one of boys. They march, girls to the right, and boys to the left. Meeting at the foot of the set, they take partners, linking elbows (Diagram 48). From then on, it is up to the leader, who is usually in the first couple, to put the marchers through different figures—many of which are similar to figures used in the "Paul Jones," or Southern Running Sets.

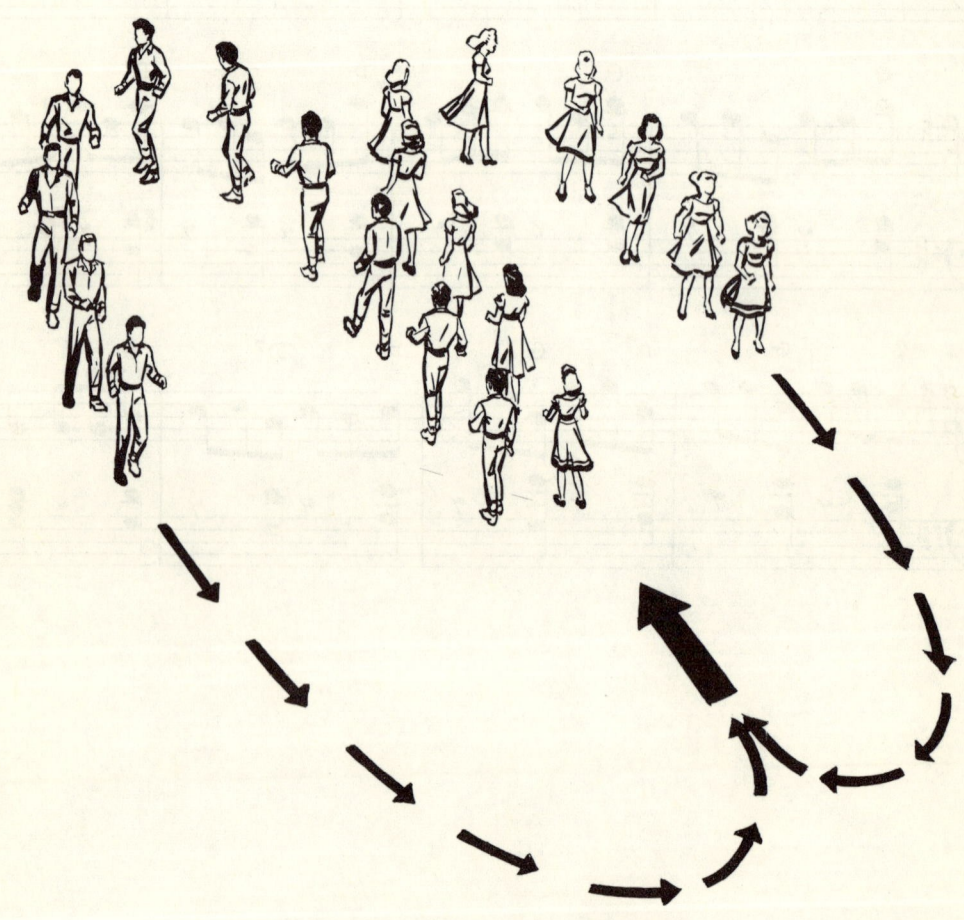

Diagram 48. The Grand March

SQUARE DANCES OF TODAY 111

Here are a number of these figures:

OPEN TUNNEL—All the dancers are promenading around the circle in a counter-clockwise direction. The first couple joins hands, turns and forms an arch, walking down toward the foot, over the line of couples. As the other couples get to the head, each in turn, turns, forms an arch, and comes back over the line (Diagram 49). When the first couple gets to the foot of the line, it turns and goes under the arch, until it gets to the head again. Each couple does this in turn, until all couples are promenading around the circle.

Diagram 49. The Open Tunnel

PROMENADE—All promenade with partners. The caller gives the command to "Move the boys up!" The boys go forward, passing one girl, or two, or three, as he directs. Each boy takes a new partner, swings her, and promenades her.

DOUBLE CIRCLE—A double circle is formed, with girls joining hands on the inside and circling left, and boys joining hands on the outside and circling right. At the direction of the caller, all reverse direction, circling back until they meet their partners.

THE BASKET—This can be done after the double circle. It is very much like "Swing Like Thunder" on page 25. The girls join hands in an inner circle, and the boys join hands in an outer circle. All are standing, facing the center. The boy stands slightly to the left and behind his partner. The boys raise their joined hands over the girls' heads and form a basket. All the dancers put their right feet in and circle left. Then they stop circling left, and "turn the basket inside out." The boys bring their hands back over the girls' heads. The girls raise their hands over the boys' heads, forming the basket again. Circle to the right now, with the left foot in.

CASTING OFF—This is usually done to conclude the Grand March. All the couples march up the center of the floor in a straight line. When they get to the end of the hall, they cast off. The first couple goes to the left, and down to the foot, as the second couple goes to the right, and down to the foot. The following couples do the same, alternating left and right. When the couples meet at the foot, they come up the center in lines of four. The lines of four repeat the procedure, casting off, meeting at the foot, and coming up in lines of eight.

At this point, the caller may have the music stopped. Since all of the dancers are in lines of eight, they need only join the ends of their lines to form square sets of four couples each!

MUSIC—It is customary to play a medley of spirited marching tunes for the "Grand March." "Anchors Aweigh," "The Marine's Hymn," and other familiar military and college songs are suitable for this purpose. The most familiar ones should be played toward the end of the march so, as the dancers go through the final formations, they can all sing together.

Chapter Seven
ICE BREAKERS AND MIXERS

A SITUATION that often presents itself for the leader who is in charge of a community or school recreation activity is one in which square dancing and social dancing* are combined on the same program.

In many rural communities there is the custom of alternating three squares with a like number of social dances. Over a period of years this has become a part of square dance tradition in these communities, and is generally accepted.

Often, too, a group may be accustomed to having social dancing on its program but may not be having too successful a time with it. Such a group will probably welcome the lively spirit and wholesome fun that square dancing provides. However, the situation will have to be handled carefully by the leader, since the members of the group may be suspicious of any new, strange activity, which square dancing would represent to them. Possibly if they knew that a square dance was being planned for an evening's program, they might not attend. The intelligent, far-sighted program chairman can easily avoid this danger by presenting the theme of the evening as a barn dance, with country atmosphere and decorations. Then, during the course of the evening, he may blend carefully-taught, simple square dances with regular social dancing.

In choosing the square dances to present in such a program, the caller should be certain that they are rhythmic and easily learned. During his first session with the group, he should leave out all complicated steps, including the allemande left and grand right and left. He should also make sure that the dances he selects are not too strenuous; and he may find it wise to do only two in a row instead of the usual three.

Occasionally a group may be very unwilling to cooperate and may have a number of factions and cliques that remain together and will not take part in the squares. If the leader sees that this is the case, he may ease the situation by introducing a number of mixers and ice breakers. These activities, making use of social dancing which the crowd is accustomed to, should serve to loosen up the participants and get them cooperating with the leader.

INVITATION DANCE

The leader asks all of the dancers to step to the sidelines, leaving the dance floor empty. Then he asks one couple to begin the mixer by dancing in the center of the floor to a slow foxtrot or waltz melody. After they do so for a few moments, the caller stops the music. Then he asks the couple in the center to separate. The girl must go to the sidelines and invite a new boy to dance. The boy she had been dancing with invites a new girl to dance. The music begins again, and two couples are dancing on the floor.

After a few moments the music stops again. The couples divide, go to the

---

*In this context, social dancing means the foxtrot, waltz, rumba, samba and jitterbug.

sidelines, and invite new partners to dance. Four couples are now on the floor. The process is repeated until everyone present is dancing. This is a very common mixer, often called the "Multiplication Dance." It is an excellent way to get a reserved, bashful crowd to participate.

It is extremely important for the caller to make sure that the dancers break up each time and "multiply," especially at the outset, and that they do not go to the side and sit down. Once they understand the procedure of the mixer, they will participate willingly and enjoy it thoroughly.

MATCHING CARDS

A useful device for making sure that members of the group take new partners at some point during the program is the mixer called "Matching Cards." As the boys and girls enter the room for the beginning of the dance, they are given cards to pin on their suit lapels or dresses. The boys' cards have words which can be matched to the words on the girls' cards. At a signal from the leader, usually midway in the program, the music stops and each person begins to search for the one whose card matches his or hers. For instance, the boy whose card says "Romeo" looks for the girl with a card that says "Juliet." The boy with "Anthony" looks for "Cleopatra." This sort of card combination is derived from the names of famous couples. Other possibilities for card combinations would be pairs of words that belong together, like "Bacon and Eggs" or "Day and Night."

As the dancers search for their new partners, the music begins. When they find the person with the card that matches theirs, they dance, and remain partners for the next few dances.

BROOM DANCES

Two types of broom dances are useful to enliven a dance program. In the first kind, one person dances with a broom for a partner, while the rest dance in couples. After a few moments the person with the broom slams it against the floor. This is the signal for the music to stop and for couples to change partners immediately. It is up to the person who has been dancing with the broom to get a partner for himself. When he succeeds and when everyone else is paired up, the one person left without a partner starts the game over again by dancing with the broom. The stunt is repeated several times.

In the second kind, everyone dances with a partner to foxtrot or waltz music. As they dance, a broom is passed from couple to couple, with the boy always doing the passing. Suddenly the music stops. The couple holding the broom is eliminated and goes to the sidelines. Then the music starts and the broom is passed again. Each time the music stops, the couple holding the broom is eliminated. This continues until one couple remains—the winner. In this game a boy must accept the broom when it is offered to him, and he must remain with his partner. Also, it is a good idea to outline a fairly small area on the floor for the dancing, or couples will be chasing each other all over the room to get rid of the broom.

CINDERELLA DANCE

Here is an especially useful mixer for teen-agers who are shy about asking persons to dance. At a signal all the girls line up on one side of the room, and all the boys line up on the other side. The girls kneel and take off their right shoe. One or two boys collect the shoes and put them in a scrambled pile in the center of the room. At a signal each boy runs toward the pile, selects a shoe, and searches for the girl who has the corresponding shoe on her left foot. When he finds the girl, he puts the shoe on her foot. Then he has the privilege of doing the next few dances with her.

HEADS OR TAILS

This is a simple elimination dance. All the couples dance on the floor. The leader stops the music and walks to the center of the floor. With his hand he indicates an invisible line across the room, dividing the dancers in half—those on his right and those on his left. He asks one member of either group to select "heads" or "tails" for his side. After the selection is made, one group is "heads" and the other is "tails.' The leader then flips a coin and lets it fall. If the coin comes up "heads," the group that called "heads" is eliminated. If it is "tails," the group that had "tails" is eliminated. The music begins again and the remaining participants dance. The music stops, and the leader again divides the group in half. He lets one group choose either "heads" or "tails," and then flips the coin as before. One half of the remaining dancers are eliminated. This keeps up until one couple remains—the winner. This simple contest requires no special dancing skills. All may participate, and considerable suspense can build up among the spectators during the final eliminations.

MUSICAL CHAIRS

"Musical Chairs," sometimes called "Going To Jerusalem," is a children's game. It can be, and often is played by adults—with great pleasure.

Line up chairs, side by side, the length of the room, so that they alternate in the direction they face: the first chair faces right, the second chair faces left, and so on down the line. The participants stand around the line of chairs. As the music starts, they march in single file around the chairs. As they march, the leader removes one chair from the end of the line, so that the number of chairs is one less than the number of marchers. The music suddenly stops, and each player sits down in the nearest chair. When all are seated, the one person who remains standing is eliminated. The procedure is repeated until only one person remains—the winner.

As in "Heads or Tails," eliminating the players until a winner is found heightens the excitement of the players and spectators and adds suspense without placing too much emphasis on the skill of the players.

ORANGE DANCE

In this ice-breaker each couple on the floor is given an orange. They place it between their foreheads, pressing their heads forward, so that the orange is held firmly. Then, as the music starts, they begin to dance. Gradually, the orange begins to slip and, in most cases, to fall. The dancers never are allowed to touch the orange to put it back in place. When the couple's orange falls they are eliminated. The couple who keep the orange in place the longest wins.

Sometimes the leader finds that several couples get the knack of holding the orange in place for a long period of time. In this case he should change the record and the tempo of the music and make the contestants dance a waltz, rumba, or a lively polka. When this is done, the oranges begin to drop quickly.

LAST COUPLE STOOP

The participants, in couples, stand around the floor in a big circle. The girls form an inside circle, the boys an outside circle. As the music starts, each person leaves his partner and marches around the floor in concentric circles. The girls walk clockwise, the boys counter-clockwise. The leader should make sure that the circles remain wide, instead of closing in in a small area.

When the music stops, each person rushes to his or her partner, joins hands, and stoops. A judge has been watching. He finds the two who were last to reach each other and stoop, and eliminates them. Then the music starts again. The girls go around in their circle and the boys in theirs. When the music stops, the partners rush toward each other, and the last couple to stoop is eliminated. This continues until only the winning couple remains.

This is a good, lively game that sometimes may become too boisterous, unless the leader keeps a firm hand on it. If there is a very large crowd dancing, it is a good idea to have more than one judge and to eliminate several couples at a time, until the couples are thinned out. Then eliminate two at a time, and then one—until one couple wins.

CONVERSATION MIXER

All the girls join hands in an inner circle, and all the boys join hands in an outer circle, around them. The circles face each other, with the girls facing out and the boys facing in. When the music starts, the girls circle slowly in one direction and the boys in the other. When the music stops, each boy is facing a new girl. Then the leader calls out a subject for conversation. The subject may be "sports," "school," "movies," "ambitions," or anything of general interest to all the participants. At once they begin to talk to each other about that subject. All talk simultaneously, loudly and fast! The leader gives them about twenty or thirty seconds to talk.

Then the music begins again, and each boy dances a foxtrot with the girl with whom he had been talking. When the music stops all take the double circle formation again, and the mixer is repeated. Each time, a new subject of conversation is given by the leader.

Through all of these mixers and ice breakers, where competition is involved, the idea of "winning" should never be allowed to become paramount. The mixers are done for the fun inherent in them, and the losers should gain just as much enjoyment in performing them as the winners.

Chapter Eight
SQUARE DANCE PHILOSOPHY

AS the square dance caller works with different groups, he is certain to encounter new situations and problems. Gradually, as he gains more and more experience, he will develop a number of attitudes and habits in dealing with these problems. These attitudes and habits, when taken together, comprise a personal square dance philosophy. This philosophy will govern the way he calls, plans a program, gains and holds the cooperation and respect of his dancers in general, his whole professional approach.

Some of the issues that will face him will be these: the development of square dance spirit, of leadership in the group, and of exhibition sets; the originating of new dances; the place of folk dancing in his program; the planning of festivals, jamborees and special barn dance parties; the working with young children and handicapped groups; the handling of publicity, costumes, equipment and facilities.

These problems exist in the main for callers in the recreation field, rather than for school teachers who work exclusively in classroom situations. However, the teacher who begins by calling for an elementary school or high school class or club often finds that he or she is in considerable demand for calling assignments in the outside community. For this reason, the following discussion should be of interest to all callers, regardless of their immediate situations.

SQUARE DANCE SPIRIT

Ideally, the atmosphere at a square dance is a friendly one. While enthusiasm is important, there should be a minimum of noisy showing-off and unnecessary "whooping-it-up." Real cooperation should be the keynote, and small, intimate groups should not remain together to the exclusion of others at the dance. When beginners come to the dance the more experienced people should help them learn the dances. It is up to the caller to make sure that friendliness, enthusiasm and cooperation prevail in his group, and to do what he can to bring such spirit about.

Sometimes this can be done by speaking quietly to individuals who in some way are offensive or anti-social. Or, if a problem arises which involves a group of people, the caller can get all the participants together to ask them what they want to do about it. Usually their solution will be a good one, and having decided on it themselves, they will probably follow through on ironing out the difficulty.

LEADERSHIP

Often when people have attended a regular square dance for a period of time and have become experts, they tend to be impatient with the rest of the group—especially beginners. They may feel that they are too good for them— and too good for the group. At this point, these people are ready to take on leadership jobs. Assuming leadership responsibility is a way for the most active, regular dancers to work off their excess energy and to make a real contribution to the group's program.

The leader should call a meeting of the most experienced dancers either before or after the dance is held. He should point out the various jobs that must be done each evening. These might include the tasks of selling or handling admission tickets, watching the door and entrances, supervising the coatroom, and preparing and selling refreshments. He might set up a floor committee, if there is need for one, to make sure that sets are formed quickly and easily, that newcomers are promptly drawn in, and that order is maintained on the floor. In addition, the leader should see that the experienced dancers have an opportunity to learn to teach and call themselves, and to practice their skills with the group. In time, when they have gained sufficient ability, they may take on considerable responsibility in organizing and carrying out the evening's program.

EXHIBITION SETS

An exhibition set is a special group of dancers who know and demonstrate difficult, "showy" dances. Sometimes the caller may use an exhibition set to demonstrate new dances to his group as part of the teaching process—and sometimes he may have them perform before outside spectators, as part of a show or pageant. A good exhibition set may put on an exciting demonstration and may help spread interest in square dancing.

Care should be exercised in the use of exhibition sets. Bad feeling may arise in the over-all group as a result of the selection of the dancers. Some people may feel that they should have been chosen instead of the ones who were and may show their resentment in various ways. The members of the exhibition set may feel that they form an "elite," superior group. If they show this in their dancing or their comments, the group may actually split apart. The choice of exhibition dancers, when it must be made, should be on the basis of regular and long attendance, cooperative and loyal attitudes, and a thorough knowledge of the dances; rather than on outstanding appearance, "flashy" dancing ability, or personal preference.

In the second place exhibition sets can be harmful in their effect on the dancers themselves. Through the ages, dance has always been divided into two types: participating, in which all may take part; and spectacular, in which highly skilled dancers perform, for others to watch. Folk, square and social dancing are usually examples of the former; ballet and modern dance are examples of the latter.

When dancers begin to think in terms of an exhibition—concentrating on costumes; working out difficult, exciting versions of the dances; and perfecting style and performance—they may lose the pleasure they once experienced in the dances.

NEW DANCES

Many people feel that square and folk dances are hallowed by age, and to make up a new dance or to modify an old one is breaking tradition. To these people, authenticity is all important. One outstanding recreation leader has put it this way: "As long as there is a wealth of fine old material for us to use, why must we create new dances? And especially, why must we use modern tunes which are completely lacking in real square dancing flavor?" The question is a pertinent one, for more and more callers are making up new squares and introducing them in their groups. Many of these squares have gained popularity and are being done widely around the country.

What is a healthy, common-sense attitude toward this question? At the outset it must be realized that dance has never been static. If dances were preserved intact from century to century they would not be folk forms, but classic dances. The very word "folk" implies that they are done by the people. And, as people do them, dances are inevitably modified from region to region and from year to year. That is the history of folk dance. Many of the dances considered authentic, genuine folk material today were created by individual dancing masters fifty or one hundred years ago. These dancing masters were the counterparts of today's callers. The fact that the dances they created survived indicates that they have real merit and are worth doing.

By the same token, if the dances created today have merit they will survive. Many years from now people may consider the dances made up today as "authentic old folk material." No one can put dance in a showcase and expect it to remain intact. All forms of culture change, and dance, as a part of culture, must change too.

Finally, the fact remains that in the ordinary square dance group, most dancers like to do new steps. They want to have the caller test their mettle, teach them new things, and give them new dancing experiences. Since they have this feeling, the caller should realize that there is room for both the well-loved and familiar old dances, and the new dances. But the important thing to remember is this: if a caller creates new dances, let them be in the real square dance tradition and spirit, and not "phony" or artificial in any way.

FOLK DANCING

Of course, square dances are folk dances too. They are the American folk dances. But, by and large, persons speaking of folk dances mean the dances of European origin—circle, couple and set dances—which employ a variety of special steps, such as the polka, waltz, schottische and mazurka. Along with square dancing, these dances have come into a considerable revival in public interest. For a long time they were done only in schools and colleges, in a few small groups in the cities, and in national halls in communities that had large foreign-born populations. But, since the 1930's, more and more folk dance clubs and organizations have sprung up around the United States, in which the dancers are of no one national or racial descent, and in which the dances are drawn from many nations. The tremendous spread of folk dancing on the West Coast is an indication of this growing enthusiasm.

Often square dancers who know little about the folk dances may be shy of them at the outset. However, once they permit themselves to try these dances of other lands, they are bound to enjoy them!

When a caller wishes to introduce folk dances into a group which has been mainly used to squares, it is wise for him to do so slowly—just one or two dances at a time. Let these dances be accepted and enjoyed before new ones are introduced. In time, the group will realize that the mastery of these dances presents a real challenge, and that they provide a great deal of fun. In carrying out the program, the caller should make sure that the folk dances are carefully taught, so that all the dancers may learn and participate rather than just a few.

FESTIVALS AND JAMBOREES

If the leader is fortunate enough to be living and teaching in a section where there are a number of square dance groups meeting regularly, he is bound to encounter the suggestion, "Let's have a jamboree!" or "Why not a festival?"

Square dance jamborees and festivals are events in which different groups join together for a big, mass dance. They are usually open to the public and several different callers may appear on the program. Exhibitions may be presented by the various participating groups; but, in order to insure the success of the event, it is a good idea to provide many and varied dances in which all the attending dancers may take part. When the separate groups perform exhibitions, the main emphasis should not be on their attempting to out-do each other. Rather, the purpose should be to demonstrate their dances and to meet together in a common interest.

A festival is usually organized around a central theme or holiday; a jamboree may be held at any time, and is usually for the purpose of bringing together all of the dancers and callers in a wide area. Colorful mimeographed or printed programs can be given out at both jamborees and festivals, illustrating the theme, if there is one, and listing the names of the participating groups and the dances.

SPECIAL BARN DANCE PARTIES

The recreation leader who is working with a teen-age or young adult group that is interested primarily in social dancing may be called upon to plan the program of a special barn dance party. Many occasions for this type of party—Hallowe'en, Thanksgiving, Christmas, a big school sports victory, St. Valentine's Day or Sadie Hawkins Day—provide special themes for the festivities.

When a party is planned for one of these special occasions, the decorations, games and activities should be centered, if possible, about the chosen theme. For instance, on Sadie Hawkins Day, the hall should be decorated like the famous village of Dogpatch. A popular event for this party is a chase, in which all the girls chase and round up the eligible "bachelors." If the theme of the party is Hallowe'en, then witches and grinning pumpkins should bedeck the room, and an eerie ghost story should be part of the program.

Decorations may be more or less elaborate, depending on the amount of time and money that can be expended; but generally all barn dances have hay, straw and ears of corn scattered about the hall. Hence, special precautions should be taken against fire. Smoking should never be permitted in a hall with decorations of this kind.

Many groups construct a ramshackle "jail" in one corner of the hall and appoint someone as "sheriff," to add to the spirit of the barn dance party. The sheriff, who may wear a big silver star, maintains "order" throughout the party and locks up those who become too noisy or rambunctious, or those who refuse to participate in the activities. The leader must keep a close watch on the sheriff, for, if he gets too enthusiastic about his job, he may have more people inside the jail than outside it.

Often a "marrying parson" will be given the job of performing impromptu wedding ceremonies. Little tin rings can be purchased in large quantities in advance. The boys may buy a ring for a few pennies or a nickel. Each time a mock marriage is held, the groom presents his blushing bride with one of these tin wedding rings. Toward the end of the evening it is customary for the girls to count the number of wedding rings each has, to determine which girl has been married the most.

During the course of the party, the leader should present a number of mixers and ice breakers like those described in Chapter Seven. Throughout the evening, he must make sure that all of the activities are in good taste and that none is overly strenuous or in any way dangerous.

SPECIAL GROUPS

Often the caller may be asked to work with groups of young children—Cub Scouts, Brownies, or children in grade schools and summer camps.

While seven and eight year old children can get real satisfaction from doing simple square dances, it is extremely important that the caller adapt his material to suit their abilities. The swing should be done as a two-hand walk-around swing. Such figures as the allemande left, grand right and left, right and left through and ladies chain should not be taught until the children have gained considerable experience. The calls should be a little slower than usual, and be made as clear as possible. Singing play parties and longways are ideal for children of this age.

The same general suggestions apply to calling squares for handicapped groups. A number of callers have worked successfully with blind groups. Other callers have gained fine results with mentally disturbed children and adults. Just as with children, the caller must make sure that his material is suited to the group. He should move them along to more difficult dances only when he is certain that they thoroughly understand everything that has been done, and that they are capable of grasping and executing the new figures.

COSTUMES

Costumes help to make the square dance a colorful spectacle and heighten the sense of enjoyment of the dancers. Usually, costume is a matter of local tradition. In most sections, the dancers wear whatever is comfortable. Clothes should not be too warm or too constricting, and the girls should wear low-heeled shoes and full skirts that will swirl about.

In some sections of the United States, particularly in the West and Southwest, men dancers wear cowboy hats, boots and suits, and the ladies wear long, frilly, dresses and poke bonnets. One set of young dancers in El Paso, Texas, used to wear cap pistols in holsters at their sides, and fire them off in a volley at the end of a square. In some rural sections, folks dress up in their very best Sunday outfits when they attend the grange hall square dance.

PUBLICITY

Another problem that often comes up and that must not be handled in a slipshod manner is the matter of publicity. A group which meets regularly need not publicize its program after a certain point if the dancers are returning again and again. However, if a new group is being organized, or if a single dance is being planned, people must be told. This can be done in a variety of ways: posters on bulletin boards around town, in store windows and sometimes strung around lamp posts, if this is permitted; feature articles and picture stories in the town newspaper; announcements on the radio; special stunts to get the dance before the public eye; post card mailings to lists of interested people. Individual clubs or organizations may be issued special invitations, to insure a good initial attendance.

EQUIPMENT AND FACILITIES

The physical details of the hall, the music, the floor and the loudspeaker system are all contributory to the success or failure of any square dance. The supervision of these details may be assigned to members of the group, but if the caller wants to be certain that they are being properly handled, he should at least check on them and make sure that the job is being done.

Many of the details are directly the caller's responsibility. If there is to be a large crowd attending, a loudspeaker system is needed which will make the calls audible to all. Whether it is his own or belongs to the group, the caller must be certain that this public address system is kept in good working order. If he has to call a dance in a new hall, he should inspect it in advance, to get an idea of its acoustical properties and to make certain that the loudspeaker will be able to cope with it.

He should also examine the size and dimensions of the hall to ascertain that if there are columns or pillars on the floor his program takes them into account. Certain dances involving circle formations or fast movement around the dance floor cannot be done if there are columns, or if the hall is long and thin.

The surface of the floor is another problem. It should be smooth—but *not* slippery! If a floor is dusted with rosin or waxed so that it is smooth as glass, it is difficult to dance on and can actually be dangerous. Finally, the caller's responsibility extends to supervising the music, whether he is working with records, a single accompanist, or a band. He must be certain that the musical accompaniment is sufficient and suitable for the occasion, for it is likely that he alone will be blamed if it is not.

Chapter Nine
PROGRAM PLANNING

THE PLANNING of any square dance program, whether it is for a school or college class, or for a community recreation group, depends on a number of factors: the age of the members of the group, their experience in dance and motivation for attending, the frequency of their meeting, the facilities available and the section of the country where the group meets.

Children of elementary school age obviously are not as capable of executing difficult steps and figures as a group of adults. Nor can they give as sustained attention to instruction. Dancing experience and the motivation of a group are both key factors in the selection of a program. A group that has been meeting for a year will learn new dances more easily and will dance longer and harder than a group of novices. The motivations of people attending a Y recreation group are certainly different from the purposes of college students in a physical education class, and would demand a different approach on the part of the instructor. Adults do not want to do mixers and strenuous dances to the same extent that a group of exuberant teen-agers do. Facilities are also important in program planning. A caller would be unwise to attempt a Grand March in a tiny, cramped hall, and, by the same token, he would be unwise not to take full advantage of the space offered him in a large, airy gymnasium. Often his choice of dances will be affected by the section of the country in which his group meets. In certain sections, singing play parties would be a vital part of the program. In others, folk dances would be expected by the dancers; and in still others, the emphasis would be on a certain type of square dance.

As he sets down the dances he intends to teach and call, undoubtedly the caller will have certain other techniques of programming in mind. He should plan to review a number of dances and figures done in previous sessions. He should include new material so that the group will be challenged and will gain the satisfaction that comes from successful learning. He should alternate the strenuous dances with less active ones, to avoid the danger of having his dancers become too exhausted. At some point in the program, he should include circle mixers so that the dancers have an opportunity to dance with new partners. He should end the session with a familiar, popular dance that all of the dancers enjoy, to insure their leaving with a pleasant memory that will carry over until the next meeting.

Since the choice of material is extremely important in program planning, a selection has been made of dances which are suitable for the various types of groups and age levels that a caller is likely to encounter.

All of the dances chosen are among those described in this book. But a number of dances in the book have not been included in the selections of material—and substitutions might readily be made. Also, depending on their background and experience, there is a certain overlapping of ability and capacity to learn among the various groups, so one dance might be suitable for several age levels.

Lists of material have been compiled for the following classes and groups: elementary school class (fourth, fifth and sixth grades); junior high school (seventh, eighth and ninth grades); senior high school class (tenth, eleventh and twelfth grades); teen-age recreation group; college physical education class; and adult square dance club.

In addition to listing the material, explanations have been given for the most advantageous use of a number of the dances. Certain dances are excellent for opening or ending a program and others are particularly useful at certain points in the program, or for certain special purposes.

The caller should not feel that he has to cover *all* of the dances listed in a single session with any one group; especially at the younger levels, he might do no more than three or four dances at a time.

It is more important for the dancers to learn a few dances *well*, and to enjoy repeating them, than for them to do a wide variety of dances without ever becoming really familiar with any of them. Therefore, in the elementary or junior high school, the teacher might go through an entire semester using only the ten dances listed here for that age level.

MATERIAL FOR ELEMENTARY SCHOOL CHILDREN
(Fourth, fifth and sixth grades)

1 Skating Away .... Circle Dance
2 Duck For The Oyster .... Square Dance
3 Hinkey Dinkey Parlez Vous .... Square Dance
4 Shoo Fly .... Circle Dance
5 Take A Little Peek .... Square Dance
6 Divide The Ring .... Square Dance
7 Hot Time In The Old Town (Version I) .... Square Dance
8 Come My Love .... Circle Dance
9 Bow Belinda .... Longways Dance
10 The Noble Duke Of York .... Longways Dance

Of necessity, these dances are among the simplest ones in the book. In teaching them, the caller should not use the allemande left and grand right and left, unless the children have been dancing for some time and are capable of grasping these figures readily. Also, he may have the children do a two-hand swing, at the outset, instead of a buzz swing.

"Skating Away" is a good dance to begin a session with because it enables the children to join hands in a circle without having to take partners, and because it is easily learned. If there are more than twenty children in the class, have them dance in two or more separate circles. The square dances chosen for this age level are all simple, rhythmic, and appealing to elementary school children. As a rule, it is not a good idea to do more than two squares in succession, lest the children lose interest or become fatigued.

"Shoo Fly" and "Come My Love" are both useful during the course of the class session, as they enable children to change partners. "Bow Belinda" and "The Noble Duke Of York" are also favorite dances for children of this age and are excellent preparation for the later teaching of the "Virginia Reel."

MATERIAL FOR JUNIOR HIGH SCHOOL CHILDREN
(Seventh, eighth and ninth grades)

1	Shoo Fly	Circle Dance
2	Take A Little Peek	Square Dance
3	Head Two Gents Cross Over	Square Dance
4	Grapevine Twist	Square Dance
5	Oh Susannah	Circle Dance
6	Sicilian Circle	Circle Dance
7	Birdie In the Cage	Square Dance
8	Form An Arch	Square Dance
9	Nellie Gray	Square Dance
10	Alabama Gal	Longways Dance

A number of the dances listed here are more difficult and more strenuous than the dances listed for children of elementary school age. For one thing there is more swinging in them. Children at this age level are better able to swing properly and gain enjoyment from it. The children are not quite ready for the more difficult folk dance steps, and so none of the dances making use of a schottische or waltz step have been included.

"Sicilian Circle" prepares the children to do the ladies chain and right and left through, which they will soon begin to encounter in square dances. "Grapevine Twist" is a favorite dance for children of this age, but they must not be permitted to become too boisterous as they dance it.

MATERIAL FOR THE SENIOR HIGH SCHOOL
(Tenth, eleventh and twelfth grades)

1	Chester Schottische	Circle Dance
2	Down The Line	Square Dance
3	Nellie Gray	Square Dance
4	Texas Star	Square Dance
5	Sicilian Circle	Circle Dance
6	Pattycake Polka	Circle Dance
7	Pass The Left Hand Lady Under	Square Dance
8	Forward Six and Fall Back Eight	Square Dance
9	Tucker's Waltz	Square Dance
10	Virginia Reel	Longways Dance

Students of high school age are capable of absorbing a considerable amount of instruction at one time; therefore the dances chosen for a class of this age level are fairly difficult and include the "Chester Schottische" and "Pattycake Polka," both of which require the learning of folk dance steps.

Since this group would probably meet in a gymnasium, the atmosphere must be a fairly controlled, quiet one. None of the squares, therefore, are of the boisterous type, nor is there a great amount of swinging in any of them, with the possible exception of "Down The Line." "Pattycake Polka" is a good dance to be placed in the middle of a class session, to make sure that the students change partners at least once. The "Virginia Reel" should be familiar to these dancers, and is a good dance with which to end a session.

TEEN-AGE RECREATION GROUP

1 Grand March .... March Formation
2 Gal From Arkansas .... Square Dance
3 Uptown And Downtown .... Square Dance
4 Shoo Fly .... Circle Dance
5 Pattycake Polka .... Circle Dance
6 Grapevine Twist .... Square Dance
7 Farmer Gray .... Square Dance
8 Bingo .... Circle Dance
9 Swing Like Thunder .... Square Dance
10 Red River Valley (Version I) .... Square Dance

A "Grand March" is a good way to begin a dance session of a teen-age recreation group, since adolescent boys and girls are often reluctant to take partners and begin to dance—particularly in a Y or canteen situation. The "Grand March" offers a convenient device for getting them out on the floor.

The square dances chosen for this age level do not require too much instruction and by and large, are appealing to teen-agers because of their lively action. They should be grouped in sets of two dances apiece, as this is found to be more suitable for groups that do not do a great deal of square dancing. If the caller finds that the young people remain on the floor, in square formation, after the second dance has been done, he can readily call one more square.

Since most of the boys and girls who attend such a recreation group want to meet a number of new partners, several mixers like the "Pattycake Polka," "Shoo Fly" and "Bingo" should be included in any session. "Bingo" is an especially popular dance at this age level.

COLLEGE PHYSICAL EDUCATION CLASS

1 Sicilian Circle .... Circle Dance
2 Captain Jinks .... Square Dance
3 Three Ladies Chain .... Square Dance
4 Lucy Long .... Square Dance
5 Chester Schottische .... Circle Dance
6 Bingo .... Circle Dance
7 When The Work's All Done This Fall .... Square Dance
8 Bouquet Waltz .... Square Dance
9 Dip And Dive .... Square Dance
10 Mexican Waltz .... Couple Dance

The dances chosen for this group are moderately strenuous, but not as much as the dances listed as suitable for the teen-age recreation group.

Squares like "Lucy Long" and "When The Work's All Done This Fall" are fairly involved in their patterns and offer a real challenge to the members of the class. At this level, the dancers should have mastered all of the basic dance movements and figures, and should be able to learn the dances with a minimum of teaching and repetition.

A good dance to end a program with is the "Mexican Waltz," since, at this age, dancers often like to end a session with a slow couple dance.

ADULT SQUARE DANCE CLUB

1 Captain Jinks .... Square Dance
2 Tucker's Waltz .... Square Dance
3 Yucaipa Twister .... Square Dance
4 Free-style Schottische .... Couple Dance
5 Wagon Wheel .... Square Dance
6 Dip And Dive .... Square Dance
7 Four In A Center Line .... Square Dance
8 Free-Style Polka .... Couple Dance
9 Forward Six and Fall Back Eight .... Square Dance
10 The Route .... Square Dance
11 Red River Valley .... Square Dance
12 Free-style Waltz .... Couple Dance

In an adult group, meeting voluntarily and regularly, it is assumed that the dancers are willing and able to learn advanced steps. For this reason, the square dances selected are among the most difficult in the book. No mixers have been included in the listing. However, if the caller sees that they are needed because most dancers seem to have difficulty in getting partners, or because the group is composed largely of single people, then he might include them at his discretion.

Often two or three free-style dances, such as waltzes, polkas and schottisches, may be done between sets of three square dances, as a sort of intermission.

BIBLIOGRAPHY

Boyd, Neva and Dunlavy, Tressie. *Old Square Dances Of America.* Chicago, Illinois: H. T. FitzSimons Company, 1932.
   Forty-two square dances with instructions for callers.
Burchenal, Elizabeth. *American Country Dances.* New York: G. Schirmer, Inc., 1918.
   Descriptions and music for twenty-eight contra dances.
Clossin, Jimmy and Hertzog, Carl. *West Texas Cowboy Square Dances.* El Paso, Texas: Carl Hertzog, 1948.
   West Texas square dances, with explanations and diagrams.
Duggan, Anne Schley, Schlottmann, Jeanette and Rutledge, Abbie. *The Folk Dance Library.* New York: The Ronald Press Co., 1948. (5 Vols.)
   Folk dances of the United States and Mexico, the British Isles, Scandinavia and European countries, with descriptions and music.
Durlacher, Ed. *Honor Your Partner.* New York: Devin-Adair Co., 1948.
   Complete instructions and music for eighty-one square, circle and contra dances, with photographs.
Greggerson, H. F. Jr. *Herb's Blue Bonnet Calls.* Box 3061 Station A, El Paso, Texas: 1946.
   Texas square dances, with descriptions, diagrams and photographs.
Kirkell, Miriam H. and Schaffnit, Irma K. *Partners All, Places All.* New York: E. P. Dutton and Co., 1949.
   Square, circle and couple folk dances, with music, instructions and some diagrams.

Kraus, Richard. *Recreation Leader's Handbook.* New York: McGraw-Hill Book Co., 1955.
> More advanced square and folk dances; games, dramatics, community singing and leadership methods.

Lovett, Benjamin. *Good Morning.* Dearborn, Michigan: Published by Henry Ford, 1943.
> Contra, square and couple dances, with descriptions, diagrams and music.

Lyman Jr., Frank. *One Hundred And One Singing Calls.* Fort Madison, Iowa: Published by the author, 1949.
> A wide collection of singing calls from all sections of the country.

Mayo, Margot. *The American Square Dance.* New York: Sentinel Press, 1943.
> Square and circle dances, with diagrams, descriptions and music.

Owens, Lee. *American Square Dances Of The West and Southwest.* Palo Alto, California: Pacific Books, 1949.
> Western square dances, with diagrams and music.

Rohrbough, Lynn. *Handy Play Party Book.* Delaware, Ohio: Cooperative Recreation Service, 1940.
> Five combined kits with circle dances, longways, singing games and simple European folk dances. Music and descriptions.

Ryan, Grace. *Dances Of Our Pioneers.* New York: A. S. Barnes and Company, 1939.
> Quadrilles and contra dances, with music and descriptions.

Shaw, Lloyd. *Cowboy Dances.* Caldwell, Idaho: Caxton Press, 1947.
> Western square and round dances, with background material, diagrams, photographs and music.

SUGGESTED SQUARE DANCE RECORDS

All records are 10-inch, 78 r.p.m., *without* calls.

Records For Patter Calls (these may be used for all patter squares in this book)

Rakes of Mallow	Capitol 10251
Blackberry Quadrille	R.C.A. Victor 45-6184
Sugar In My Coffee-O	Kismet SD-3
Limber Jim	Windsor 7109-A

Records For Singing Calls In This Book

Red River Valley	Windsor 7129-B
Hot Time In The Old Town	Windsor 7115-B
Darling Nellie Gray	Imperial 1011
Hinkey Dinkey Parlez Vous	Folkraft F1059B
Golden Slippers	Folkraft F-1314A (add circle left and right introduction)
Camptown Races	Folkraft F1069A (eliminate introduction)
Red Wing	MacGregor 640-B
My Pretty Girl (for Tucker's Waltz)	Windsor 7112-A

SQUARE DANCES OF TODAY

Life On The Ocean Wave	Coral 64035
Lucy Long	Folk Dancer MH-1042-A
When The Work's All Done This Fall	Folkraft F1059A

Records For Other Dances

Shoo Fly	Folk Dancer MH-1108-B
Oh Susannah	R.C.A. Victor 45-6178 (add swing, before promenade)
Come My Love	Folk Dancer MH-1110-A (tune of "Oats, Peas, Beans")
Bingo	R.C.A. Victor 45-6172
Chester Schottische	Any good schottische: R.C.A. Victor 45-6177
Buffalo Gals	Coral 64035
Mexican Waltz	Folk Dancer MH-1016-A
Sicilian Circle	Blackberry Quadrille (listed earlier) may be used
Virginia Reel	R.C.A. Victor 45-6180

Square Dance and Play Party Records With Calls and Direction Booklets

R.C.A. Victor "Let's Square Dance Series," by Richard Kraus. This series consists of five albums, available in 45, 33⅓ and 78 r.p.m., of graded dances, suitable for groups or classes from third grade through high school.

SQUARE AND FOLK DANCE PERIODICALS

American Squares, Newark, N. J.
Sets In Order, Los Angeles, Cal.
Viltis, San Diego, Cal.

These publications carry up-to-date news of square dance camps, summer schools, festivals, and special workshops.

Square dance books and records may be purchased through:
Ed Kremer's Folk Shop, San Francisco, Cal.
American Squares Book and Record Shop, Newark, N. J.
Folk Dance House, New York, N. Y.
Kismet Record Shop, New York, N. Y.